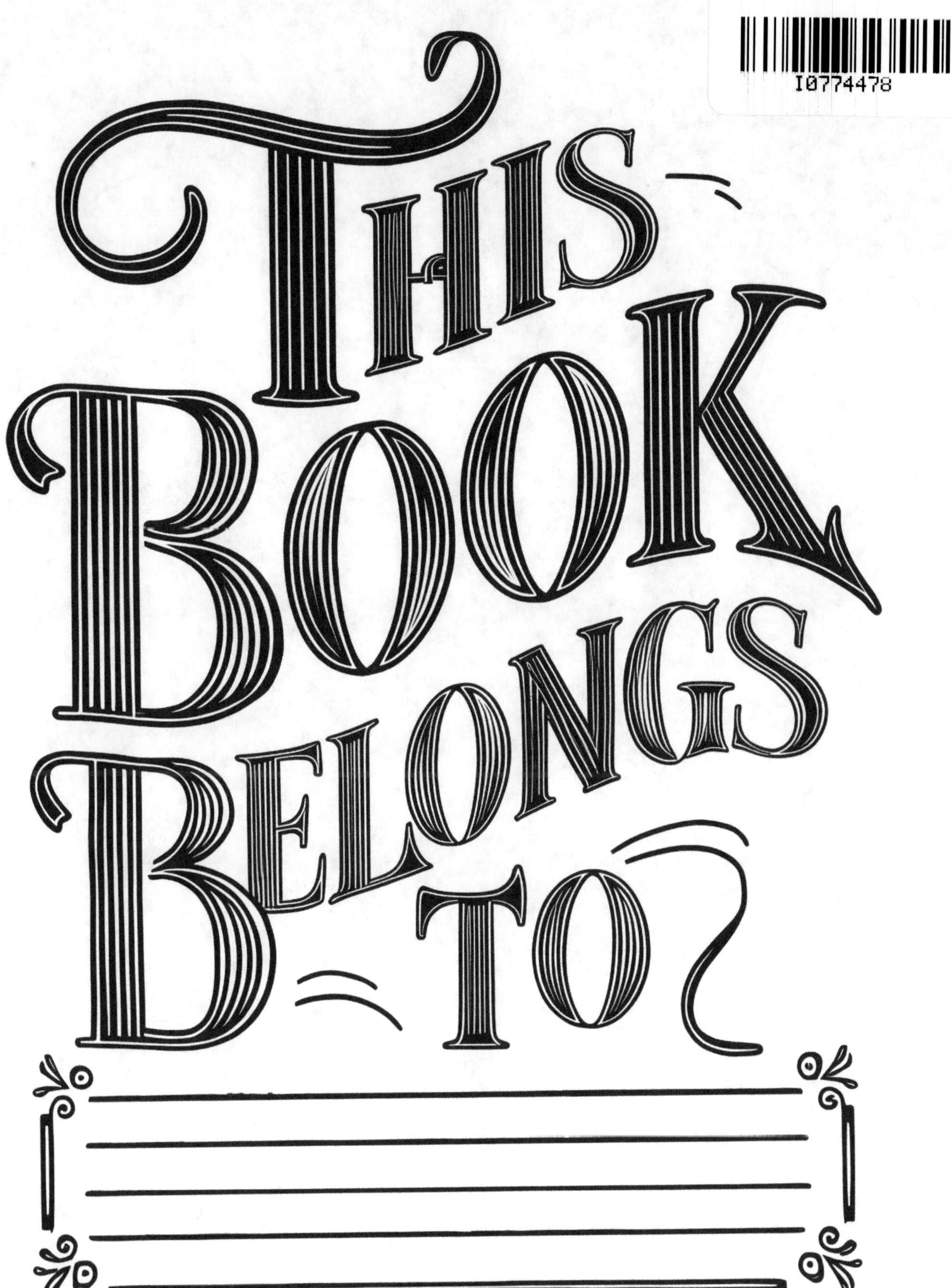

THIS BOOK BELONGS TO

COLOR TESTER

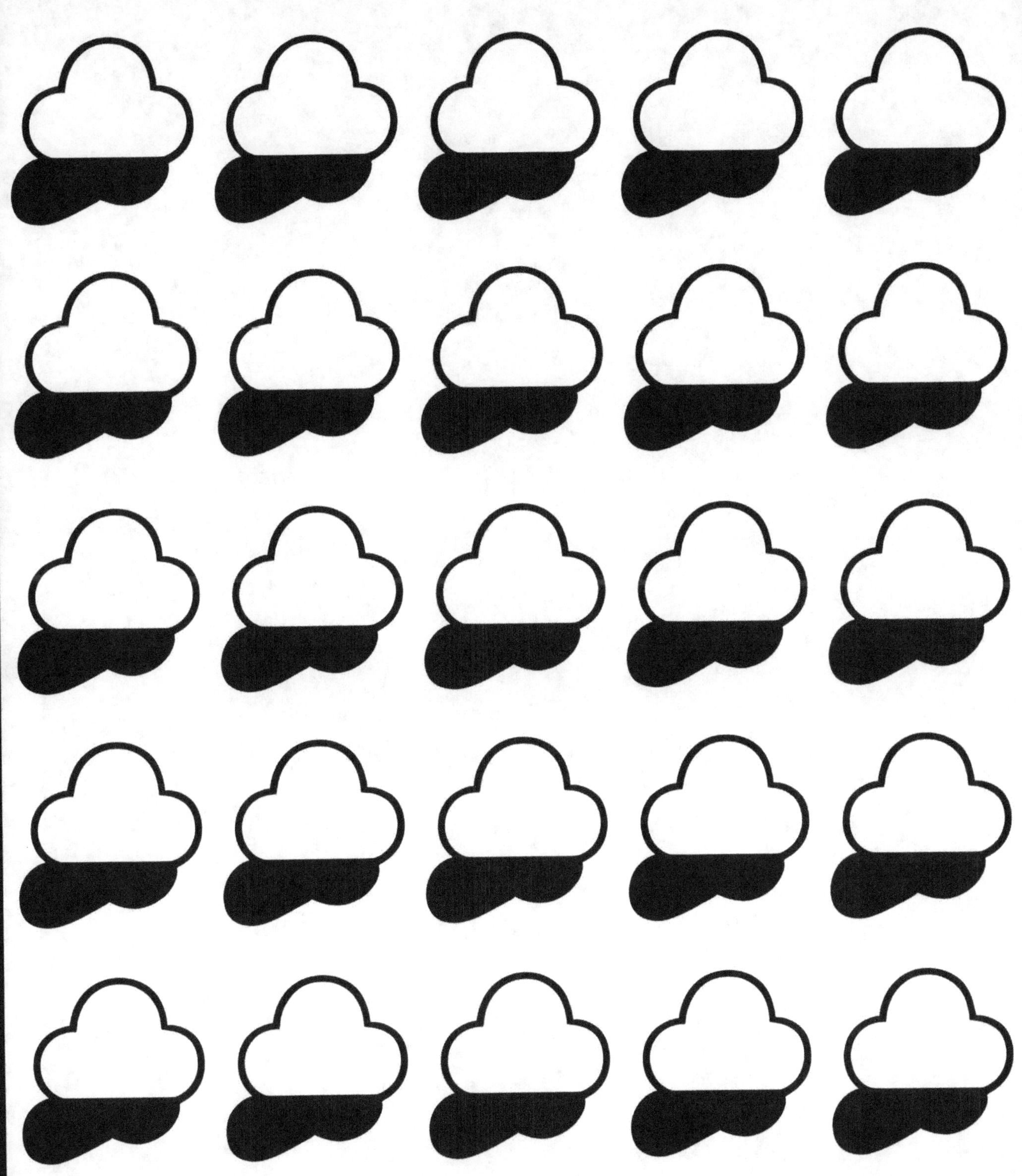

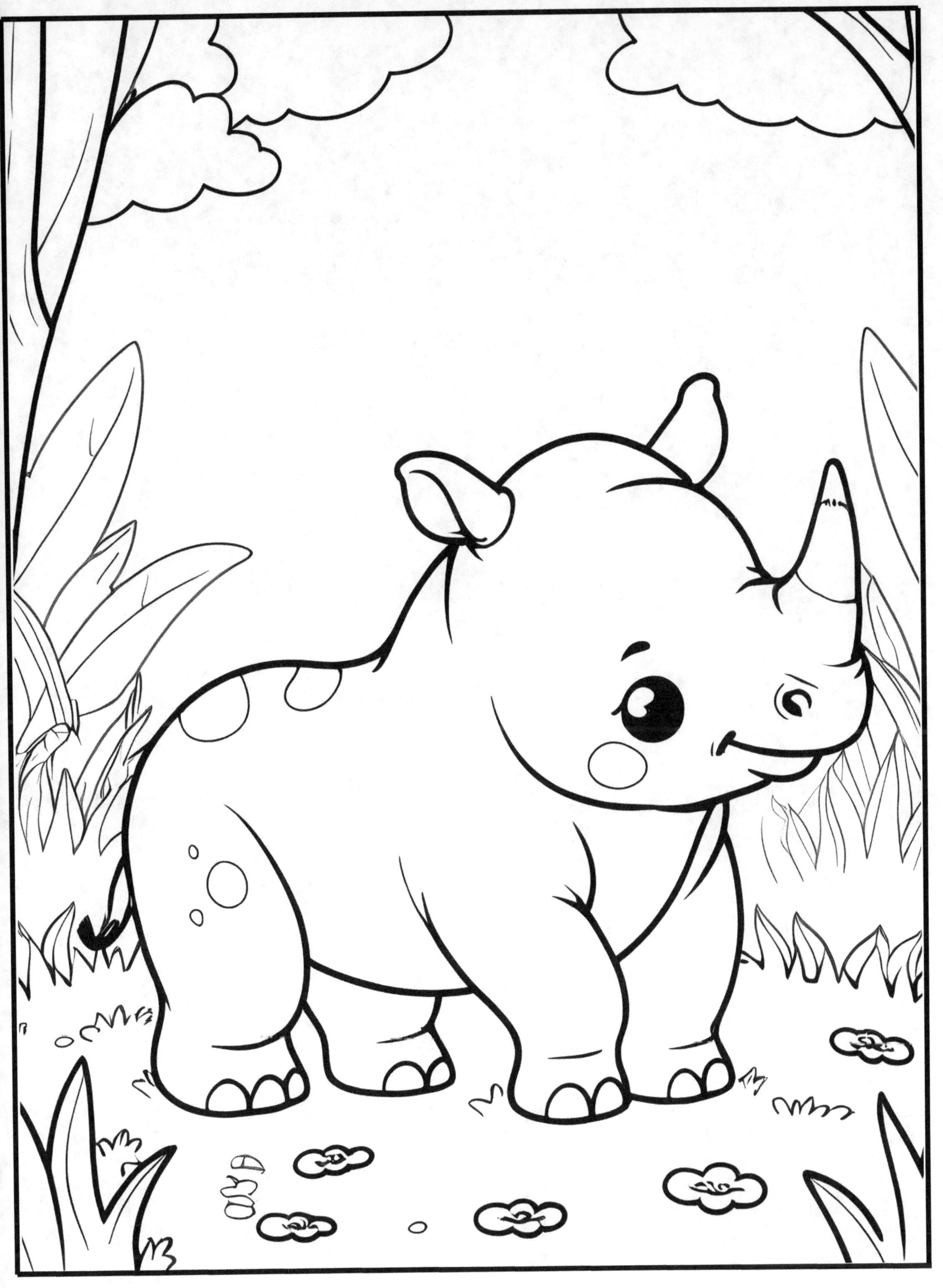

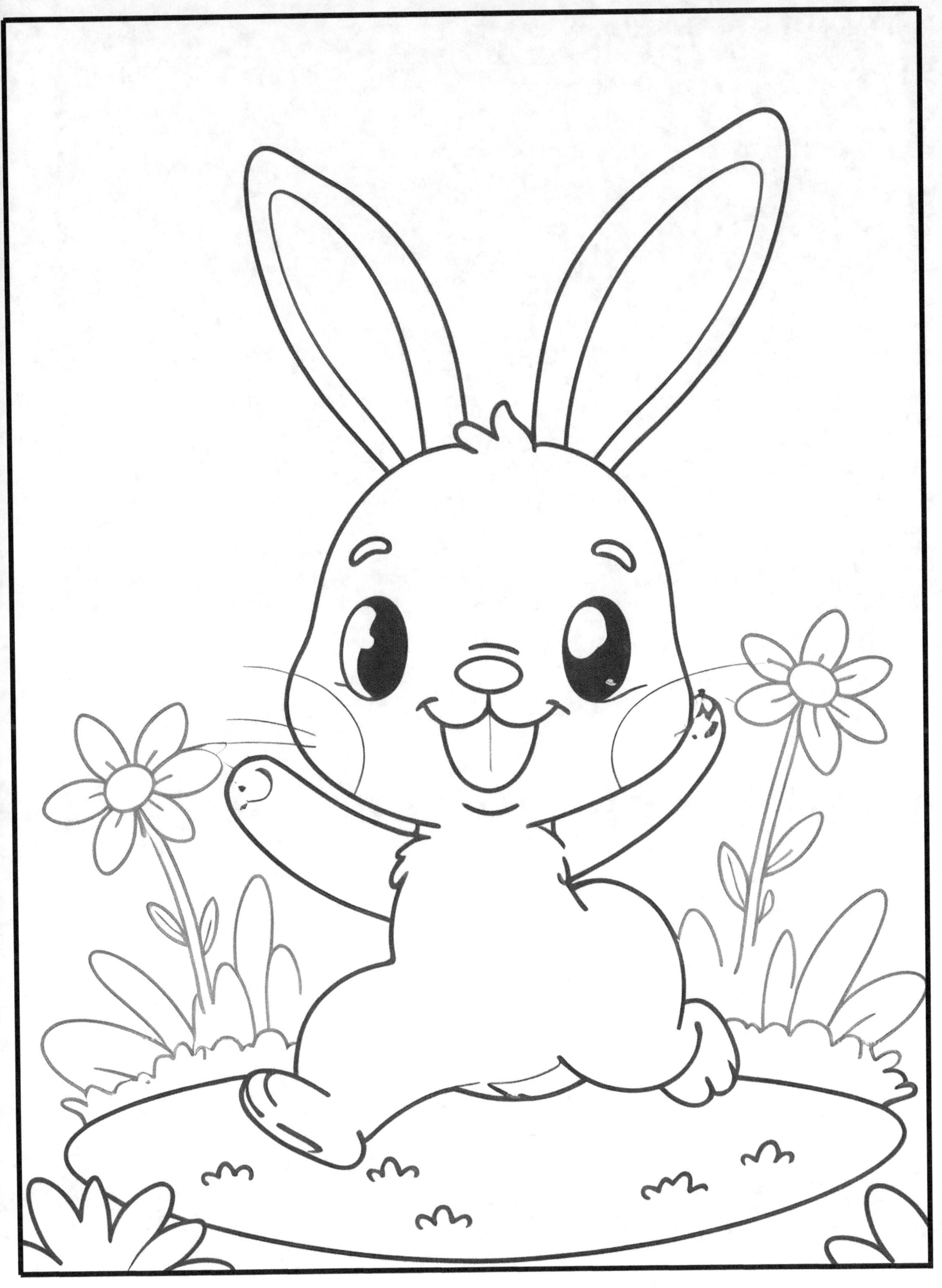

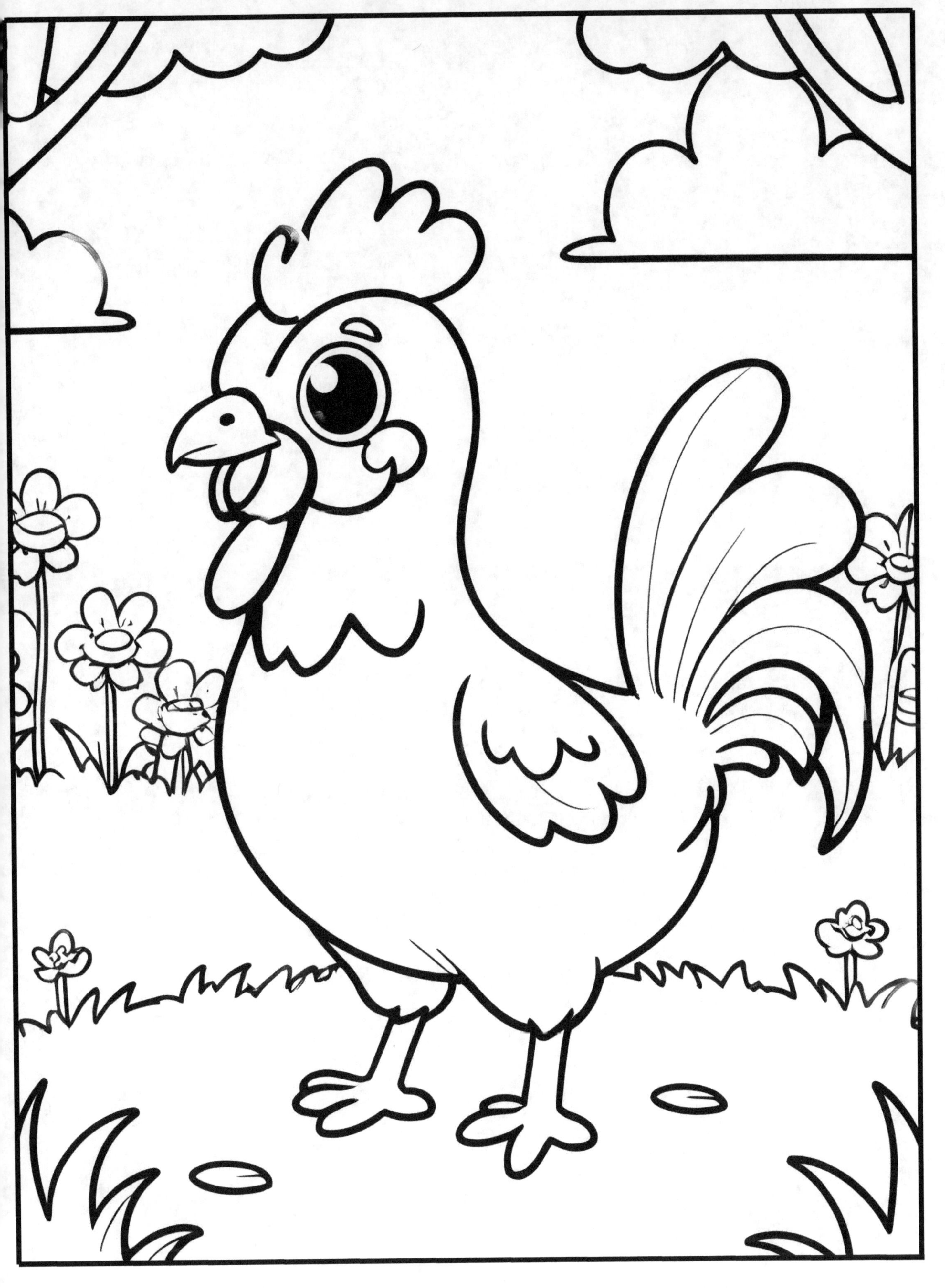

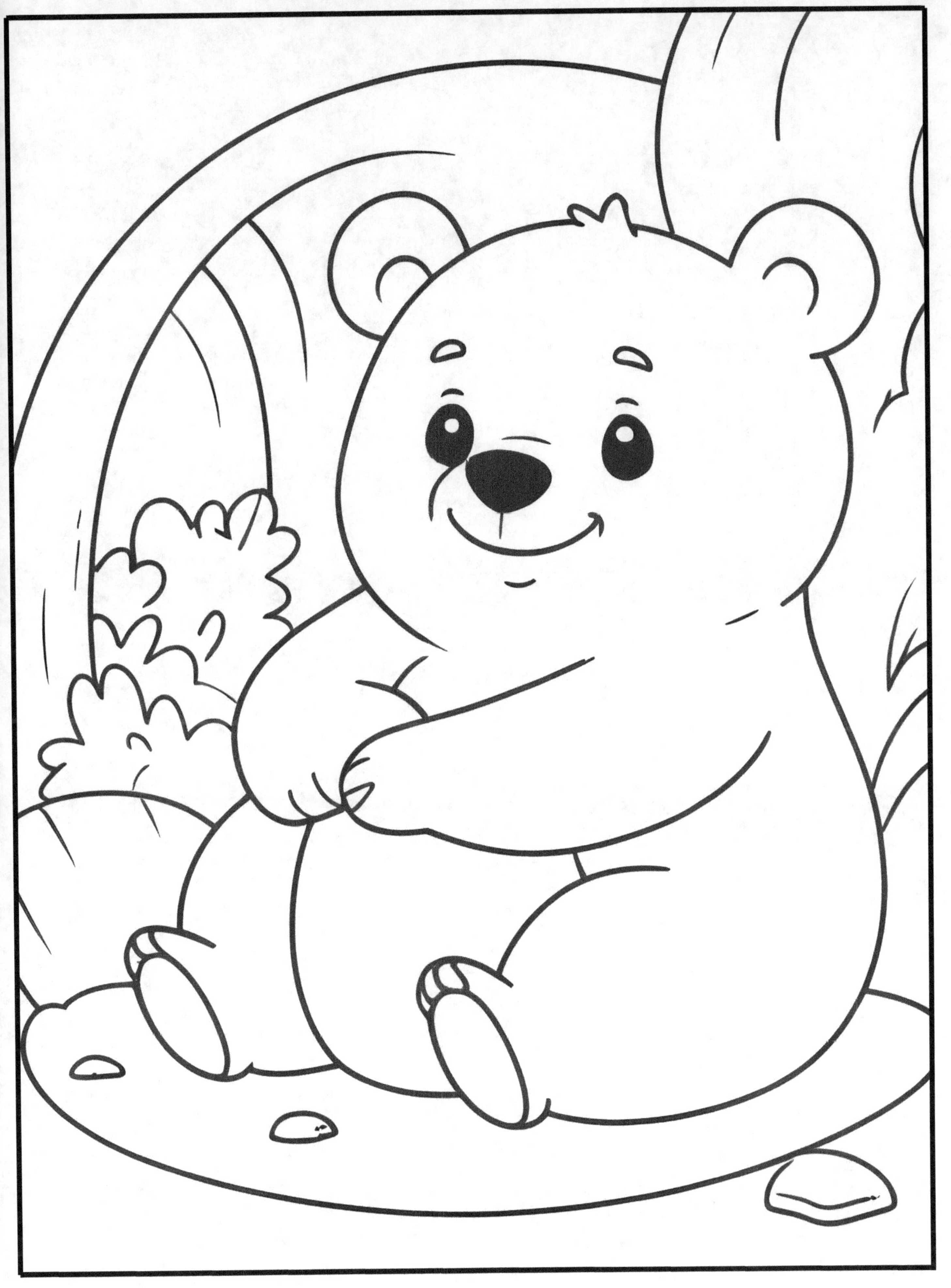

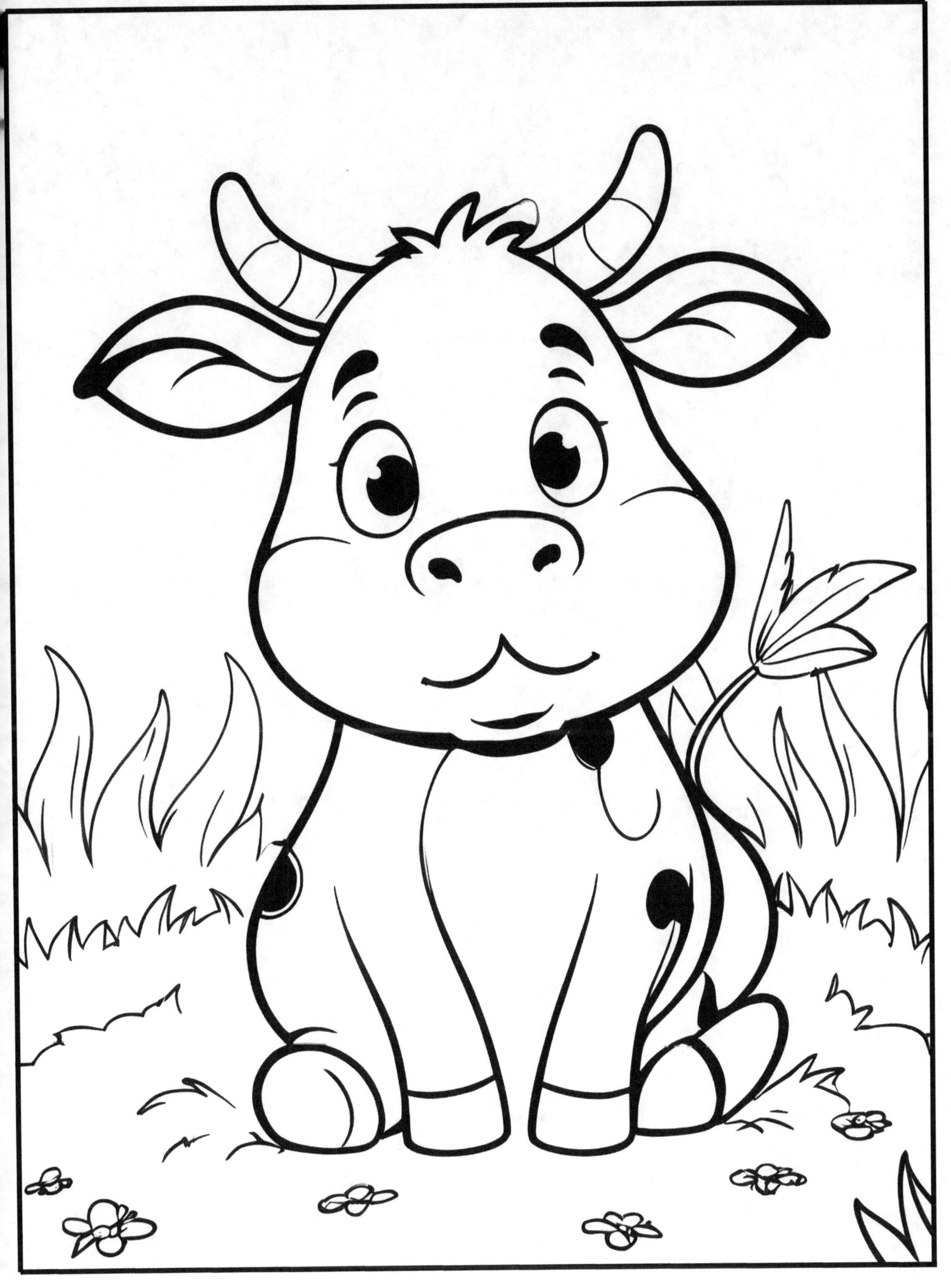

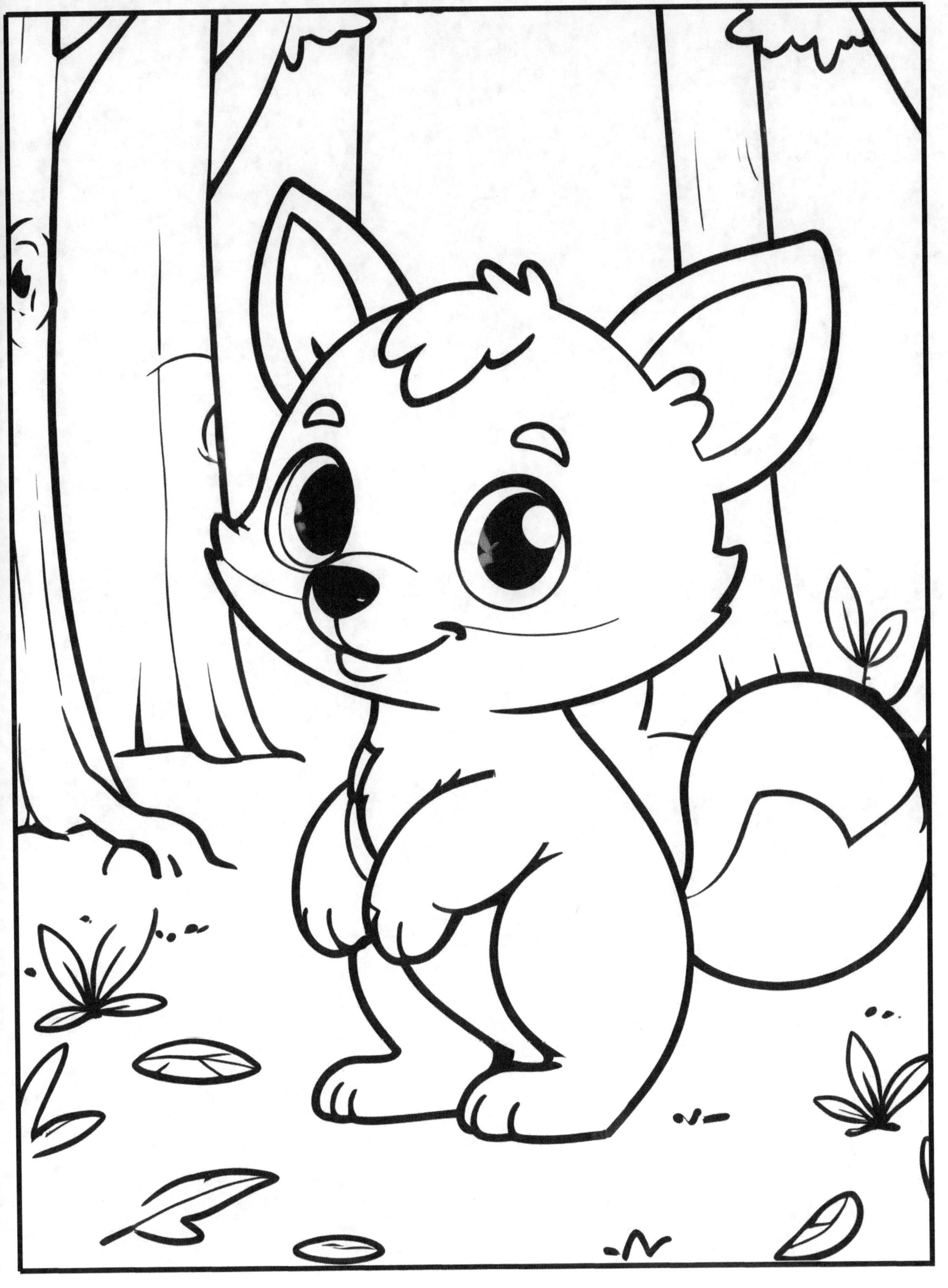

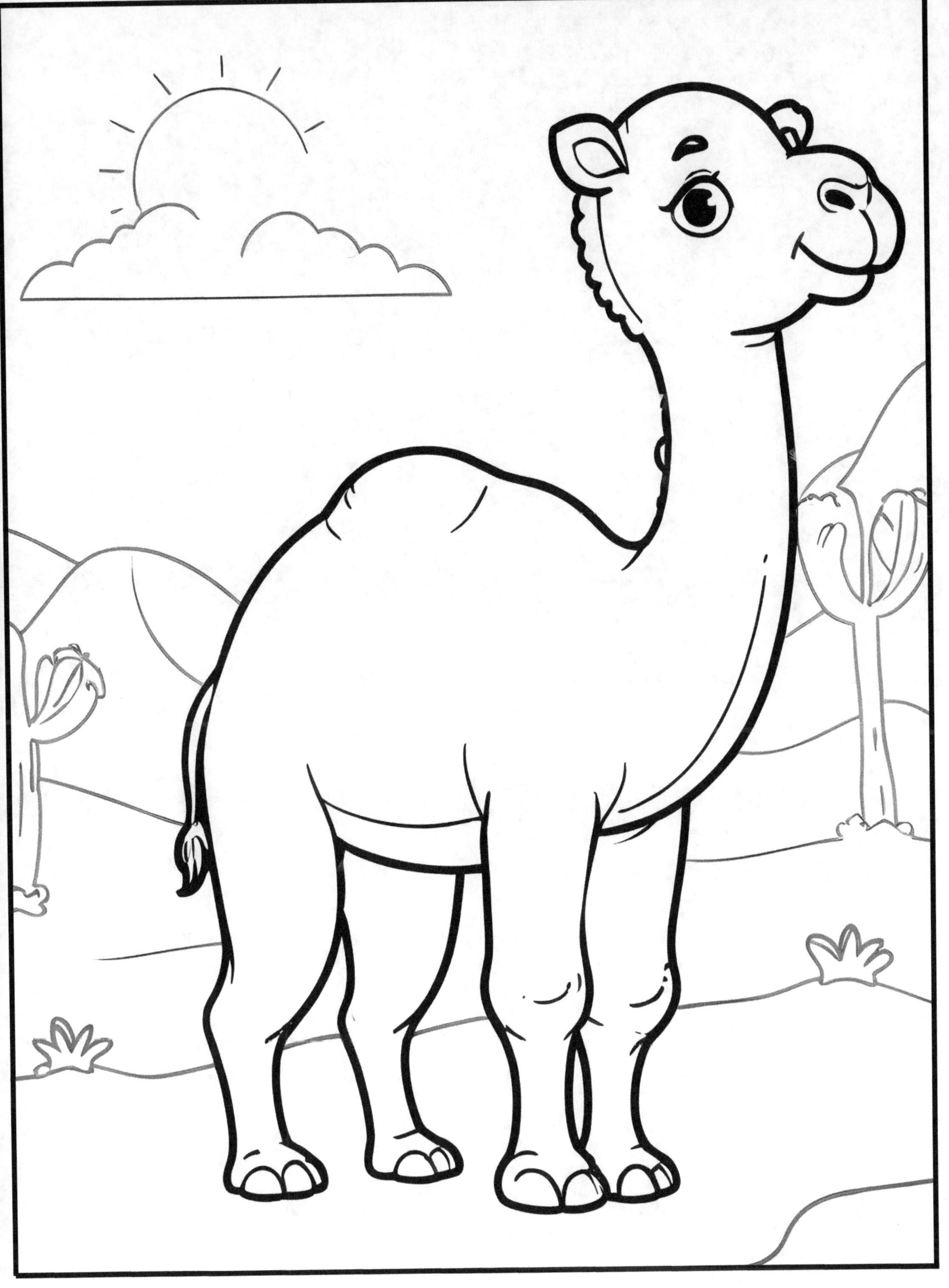

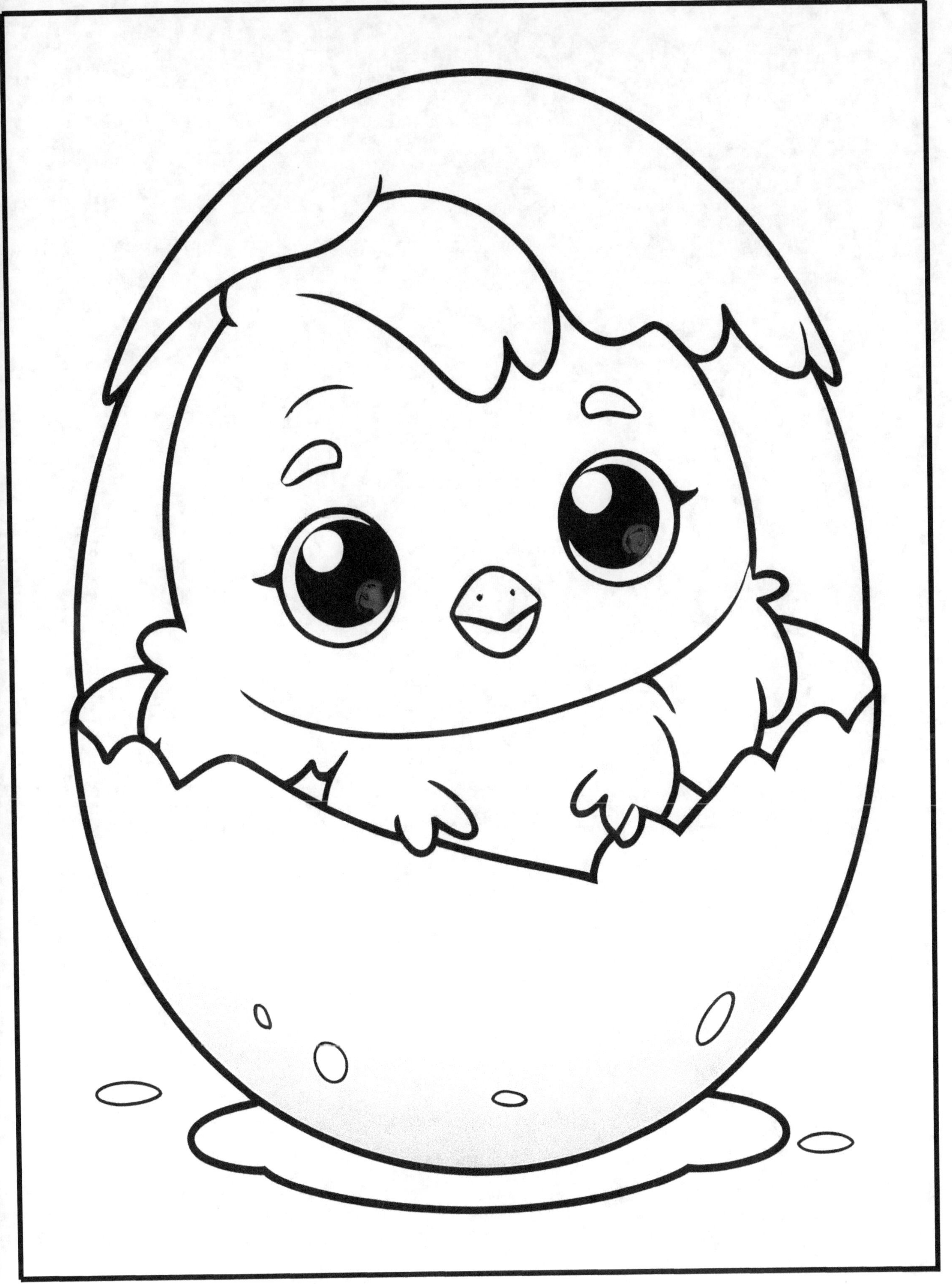

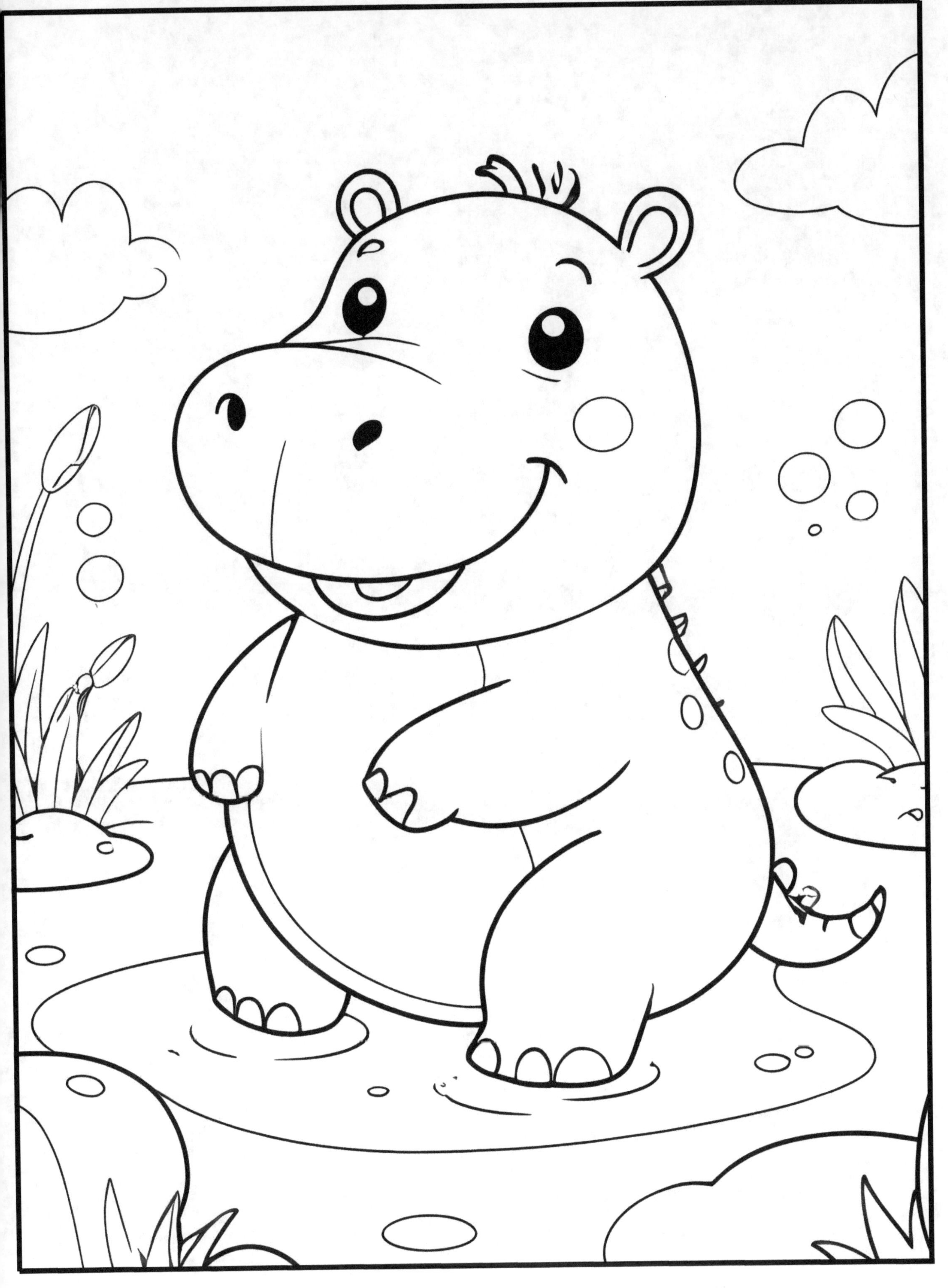

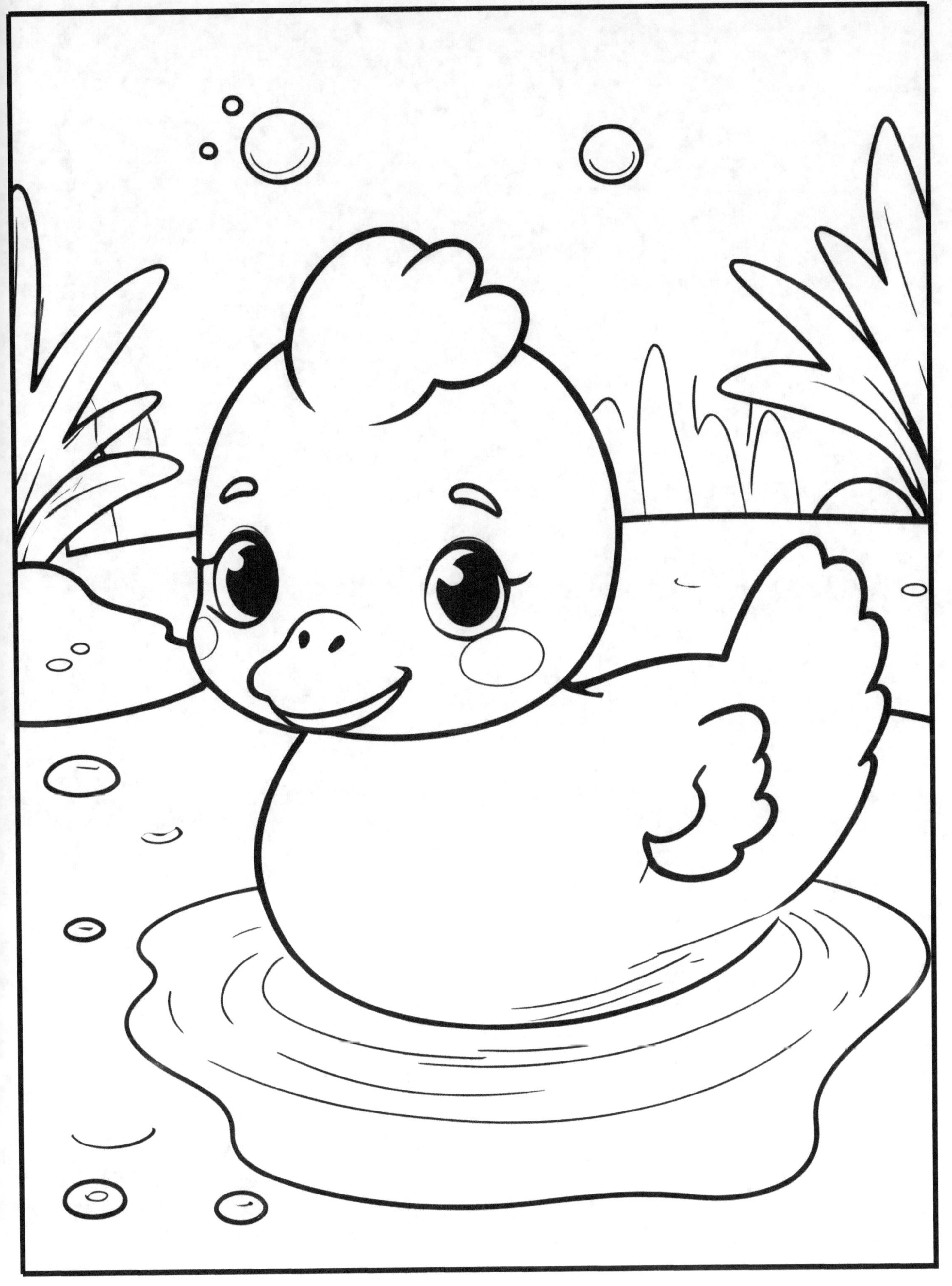

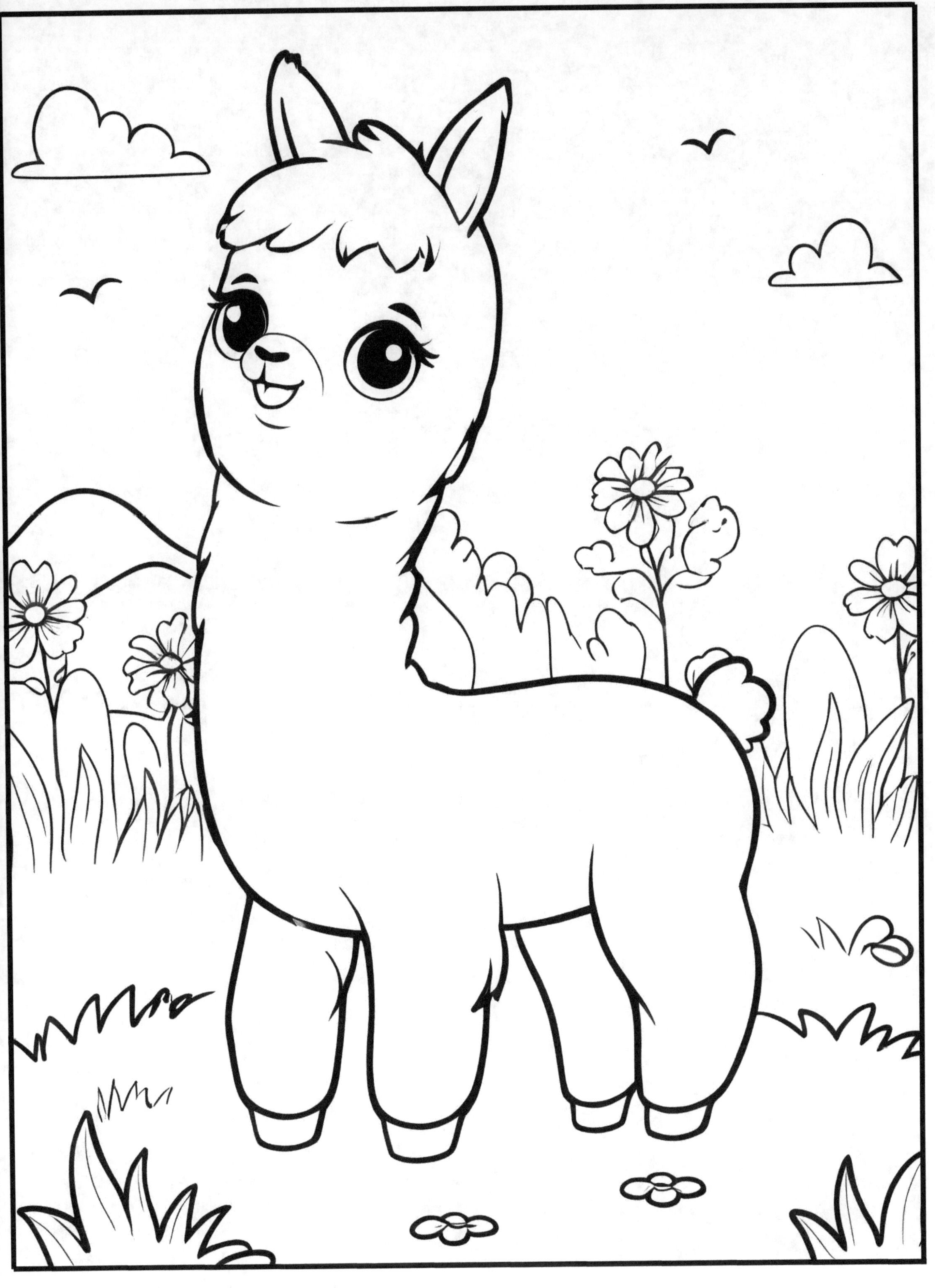

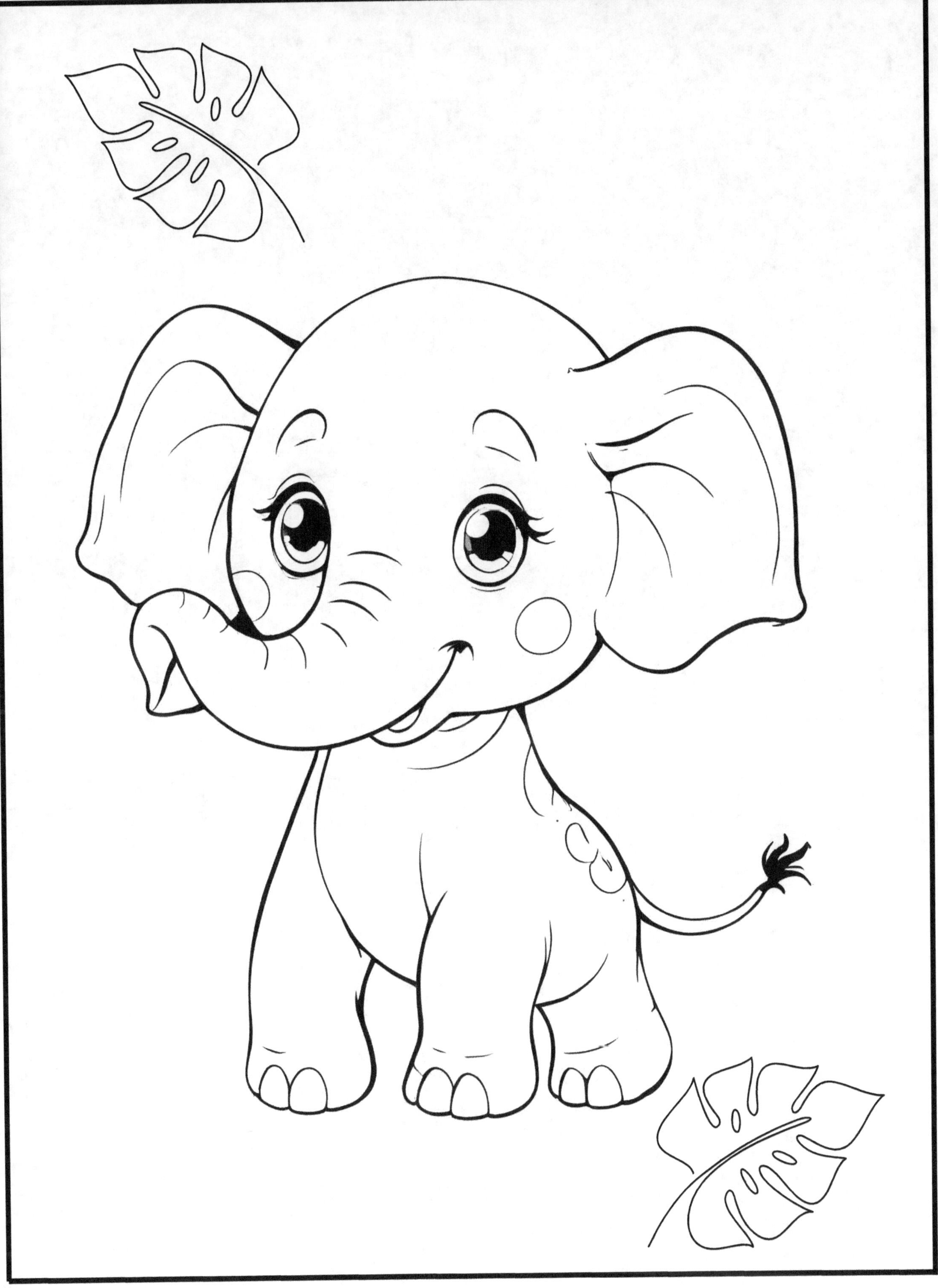

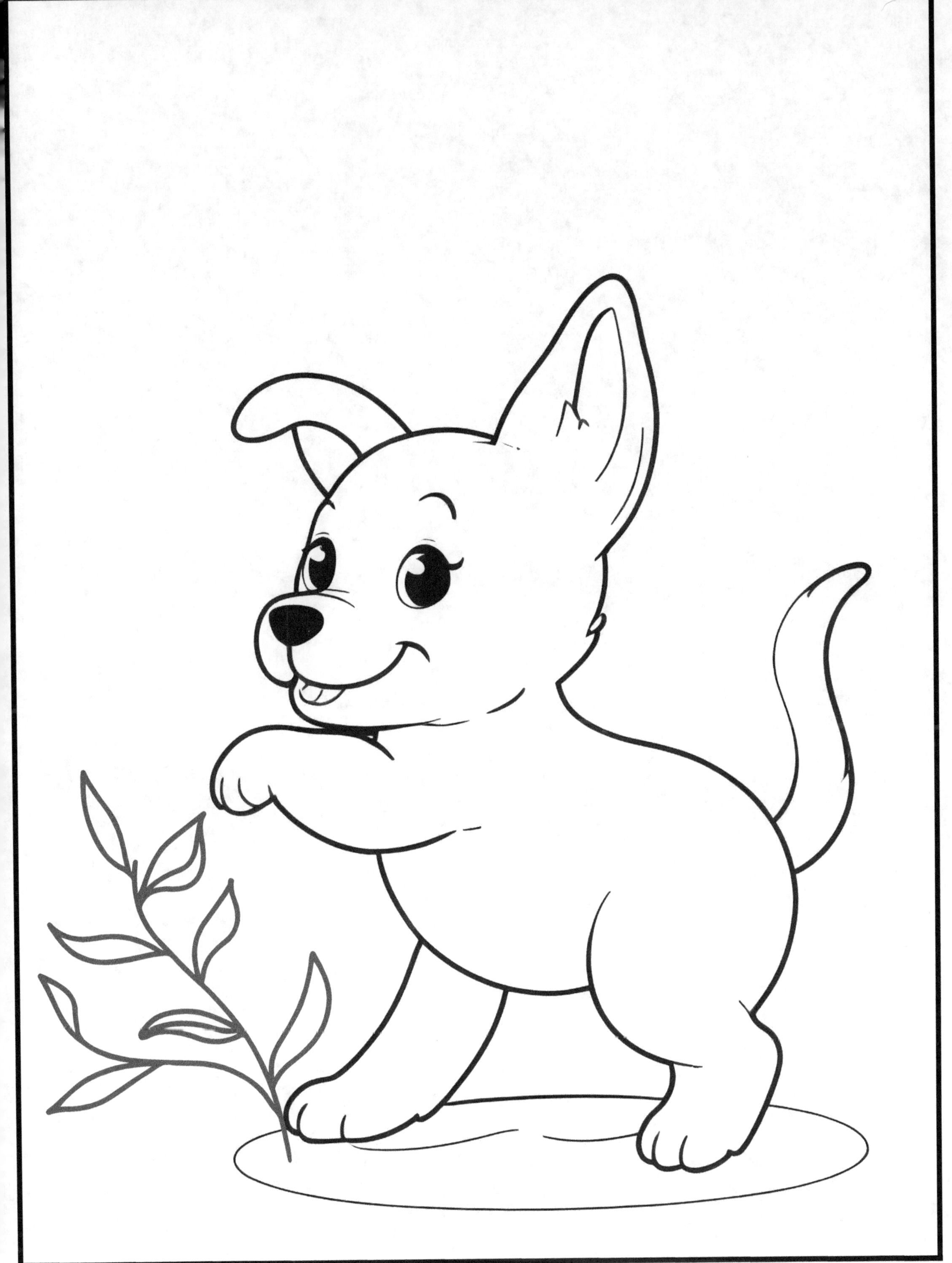

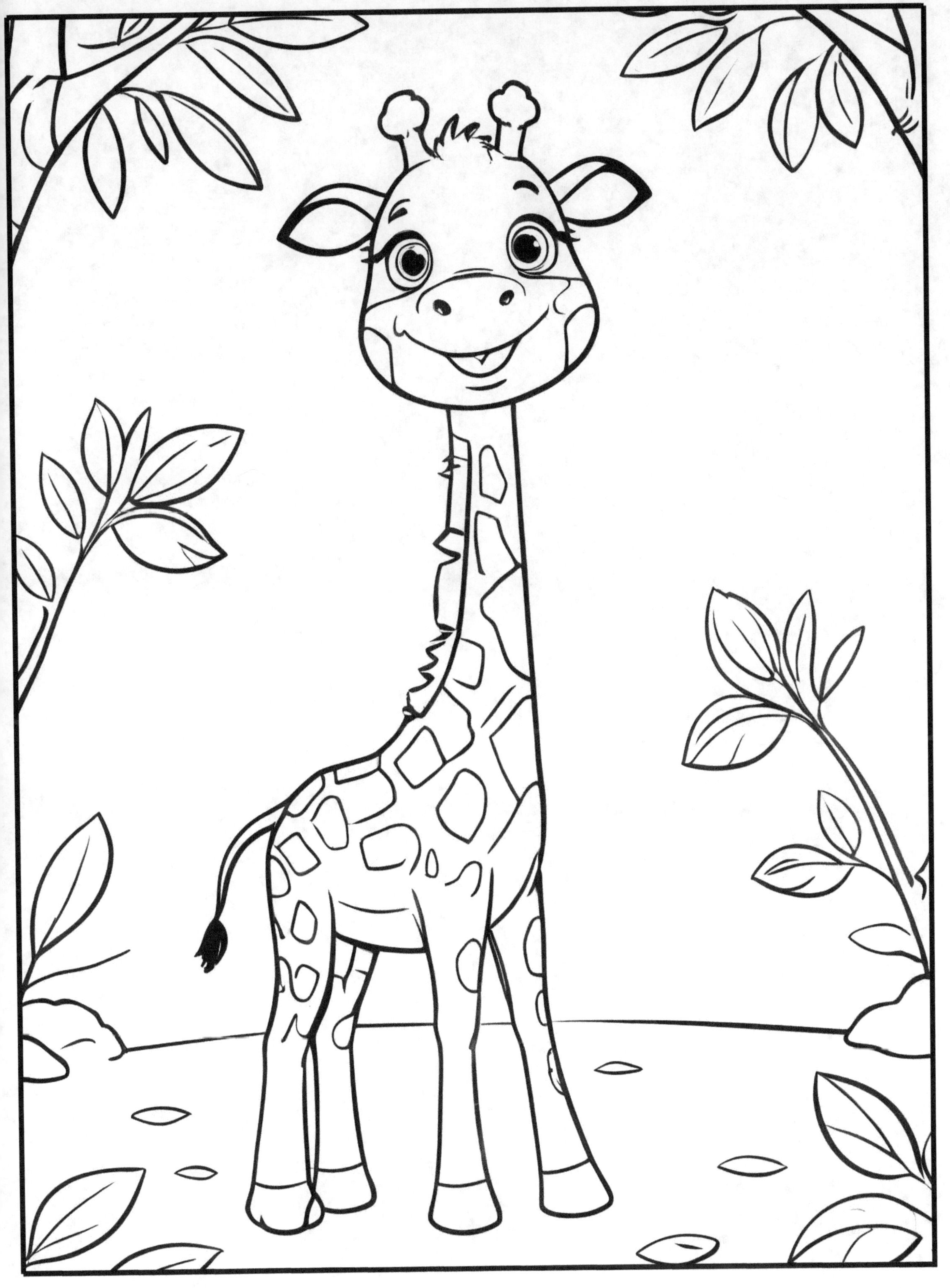

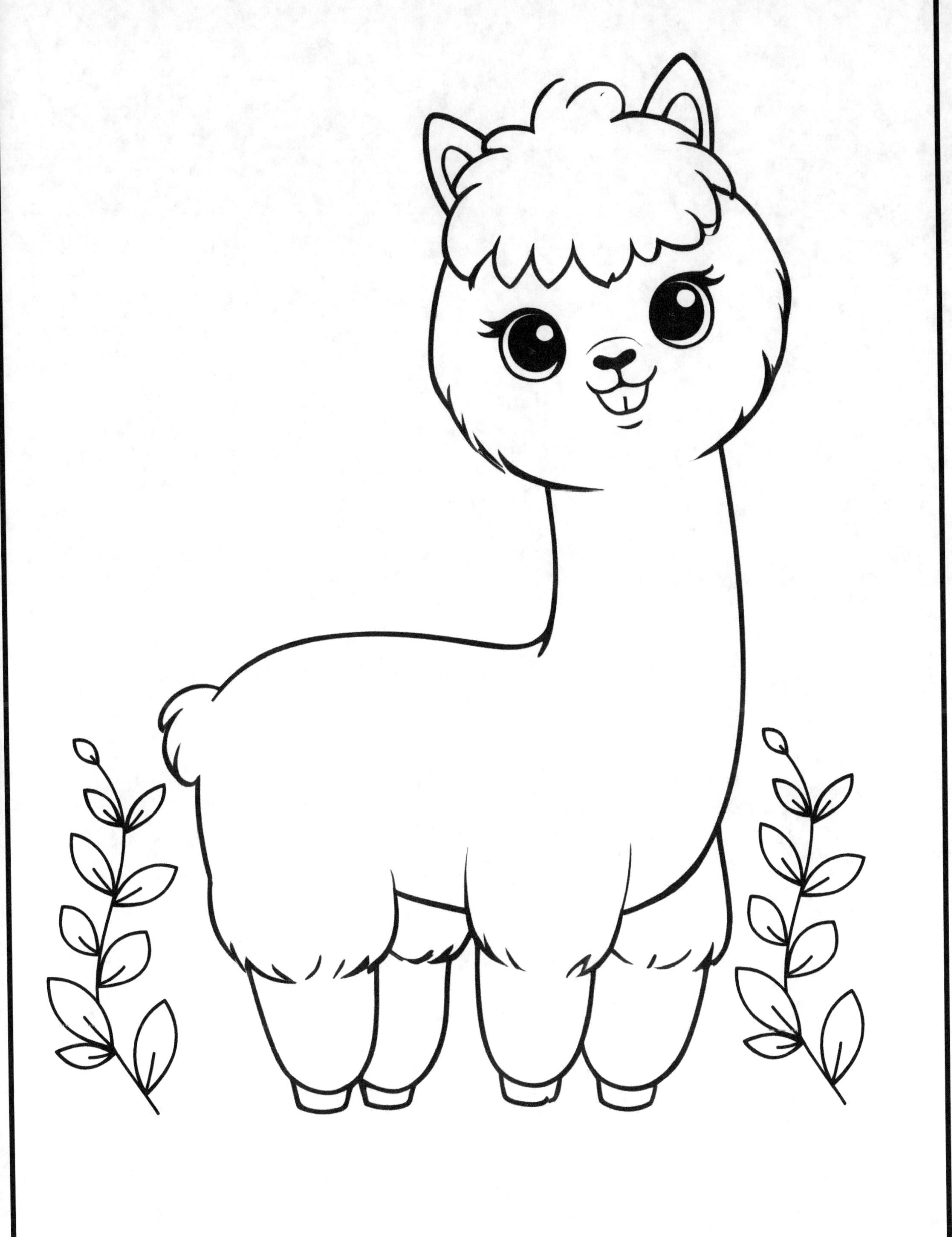

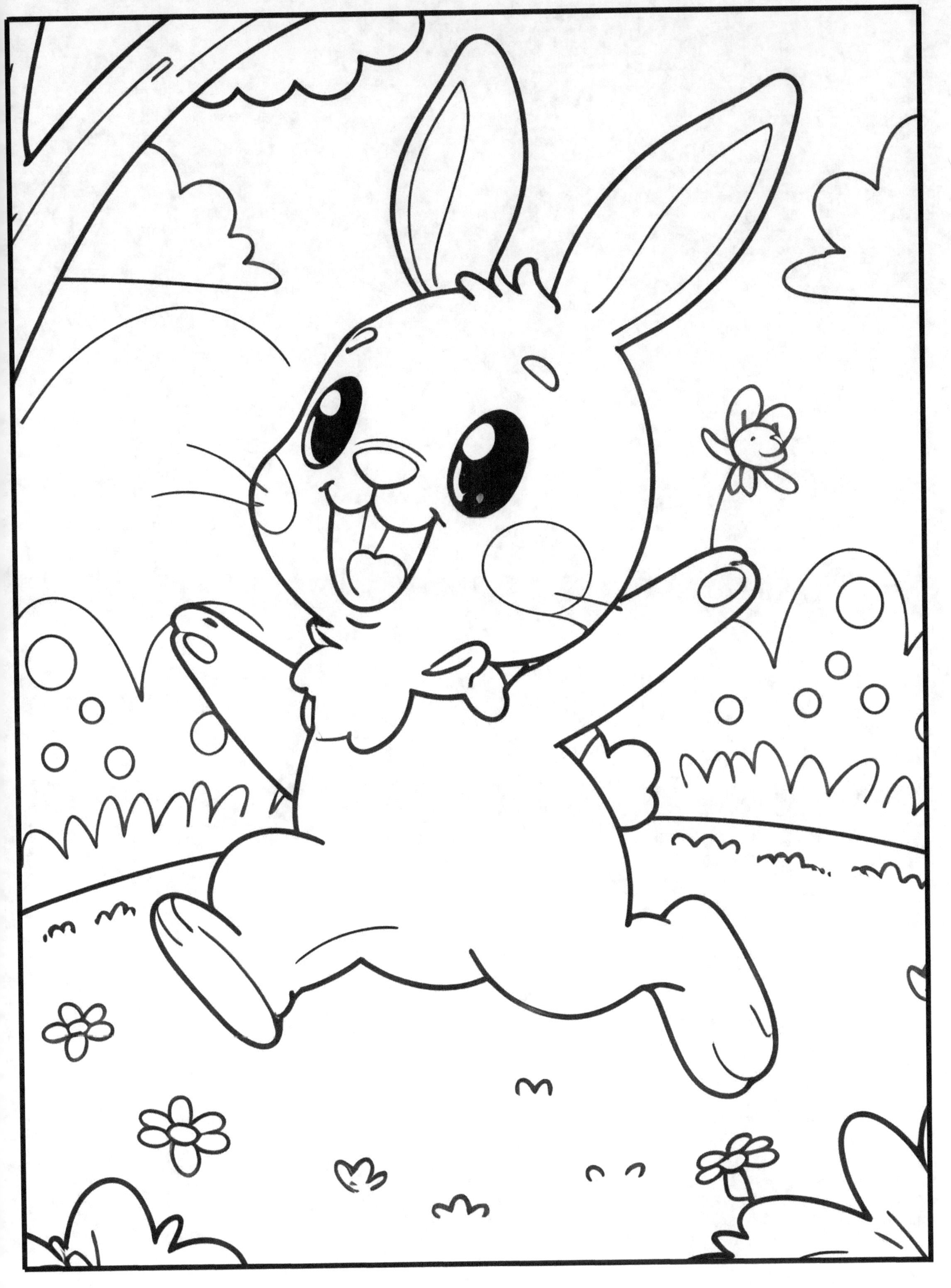

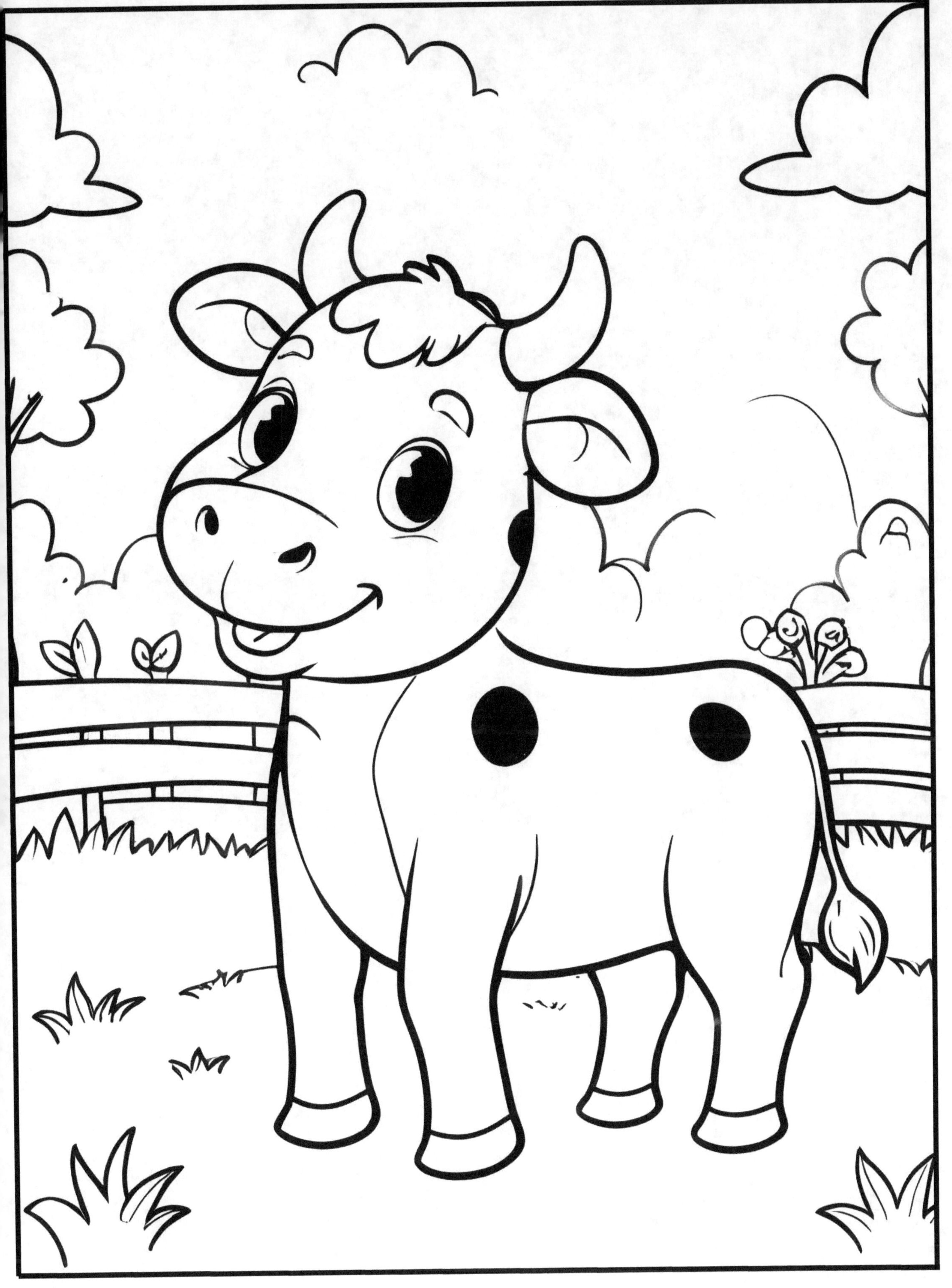

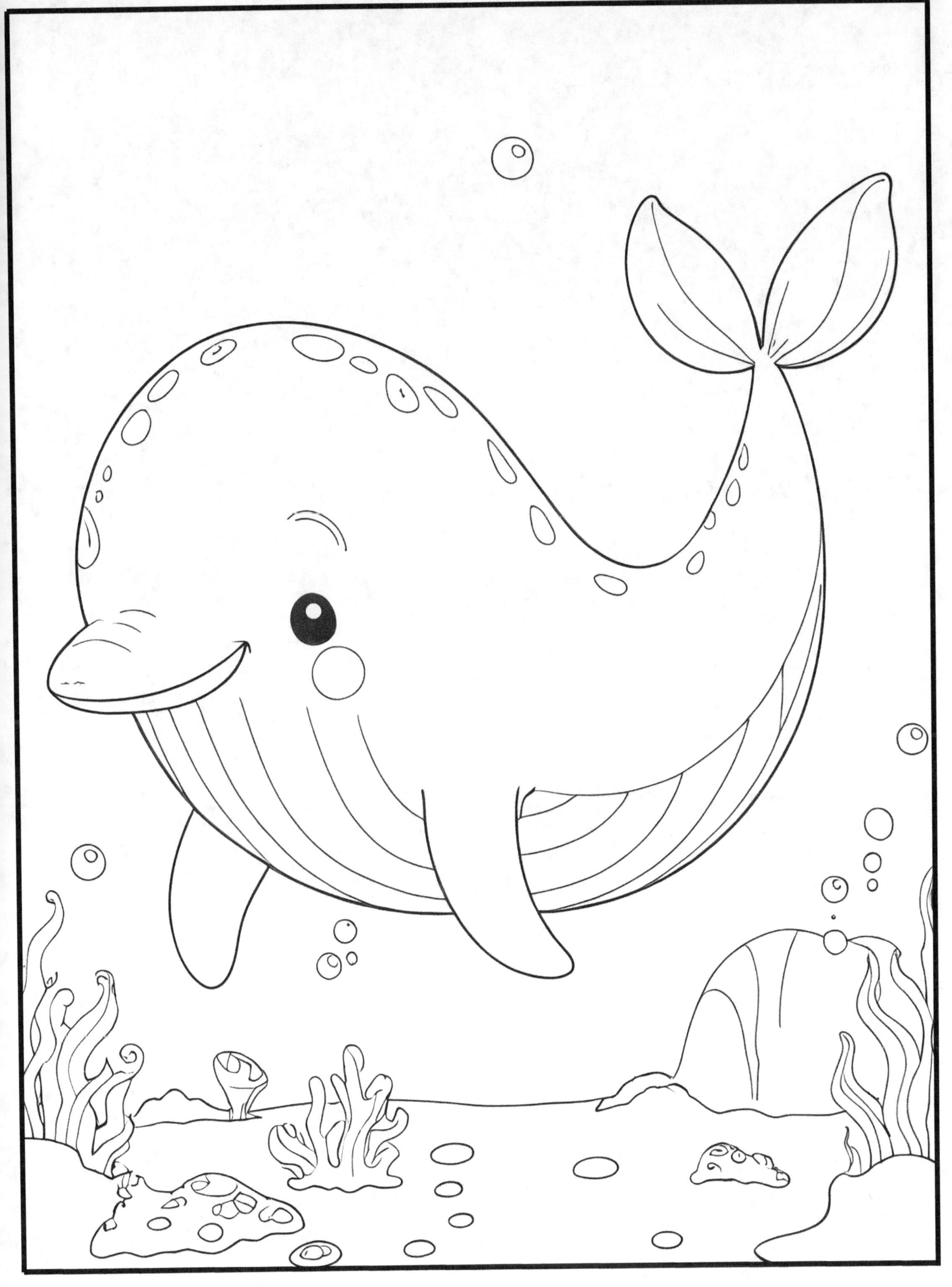

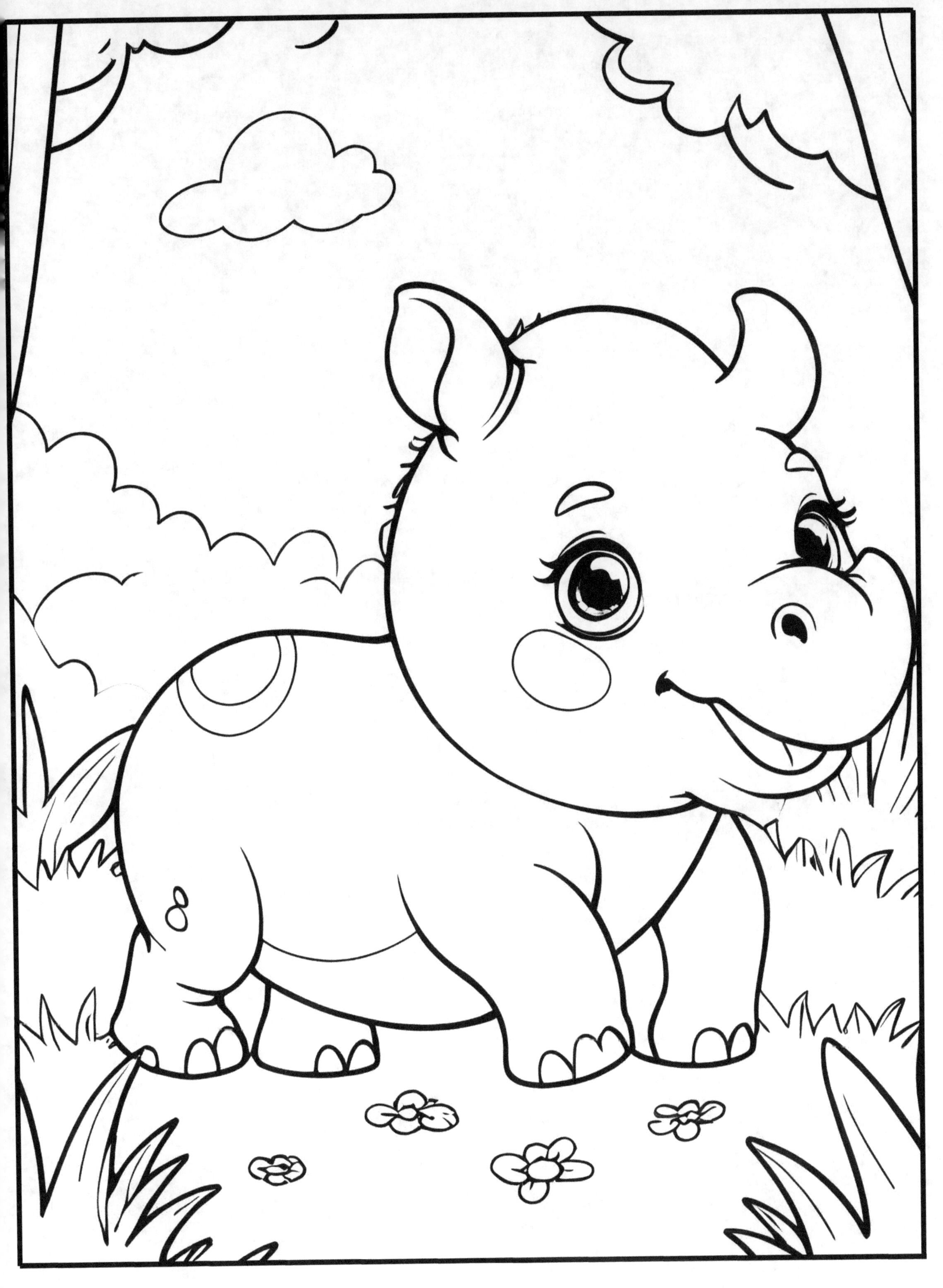

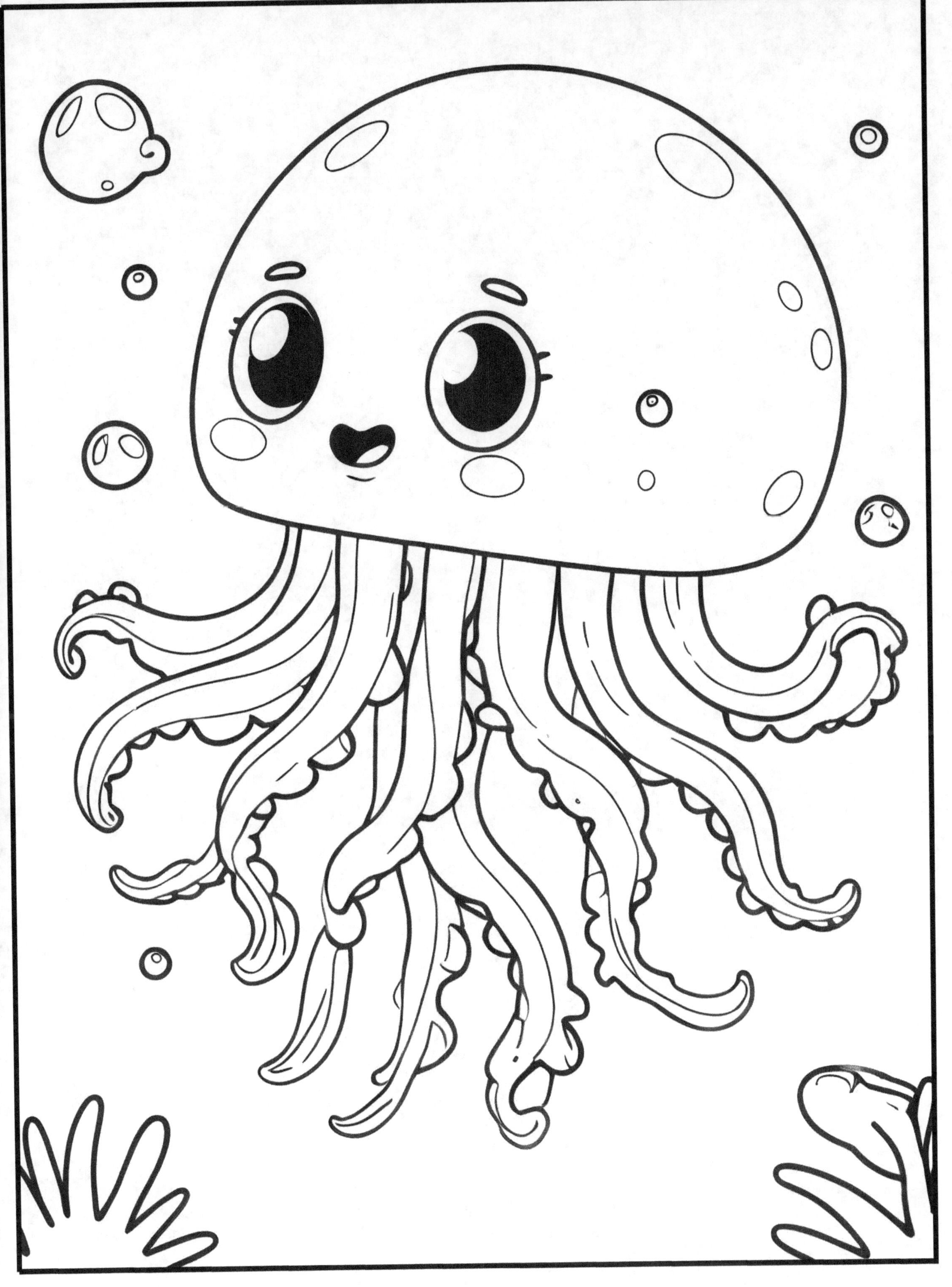

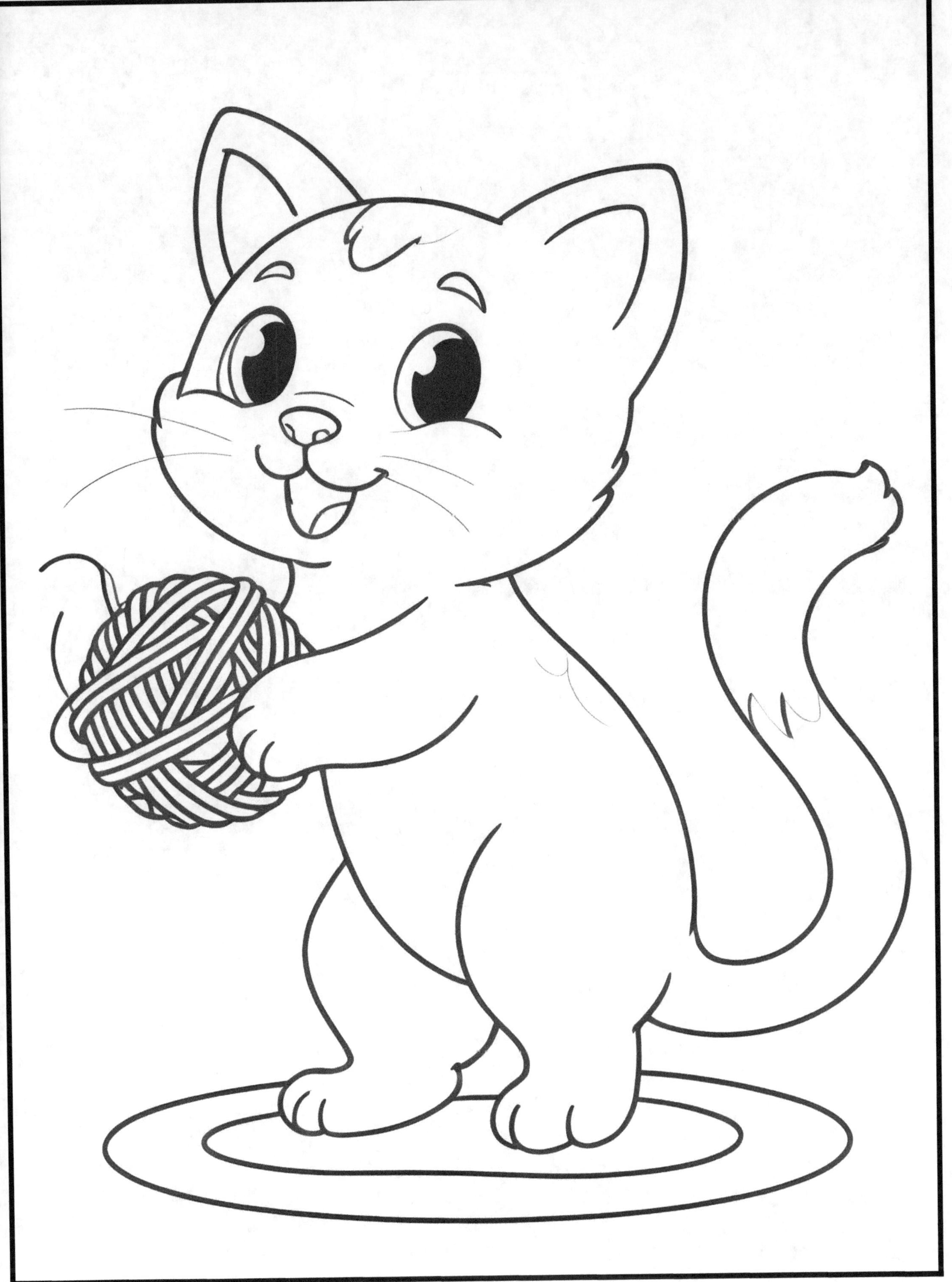

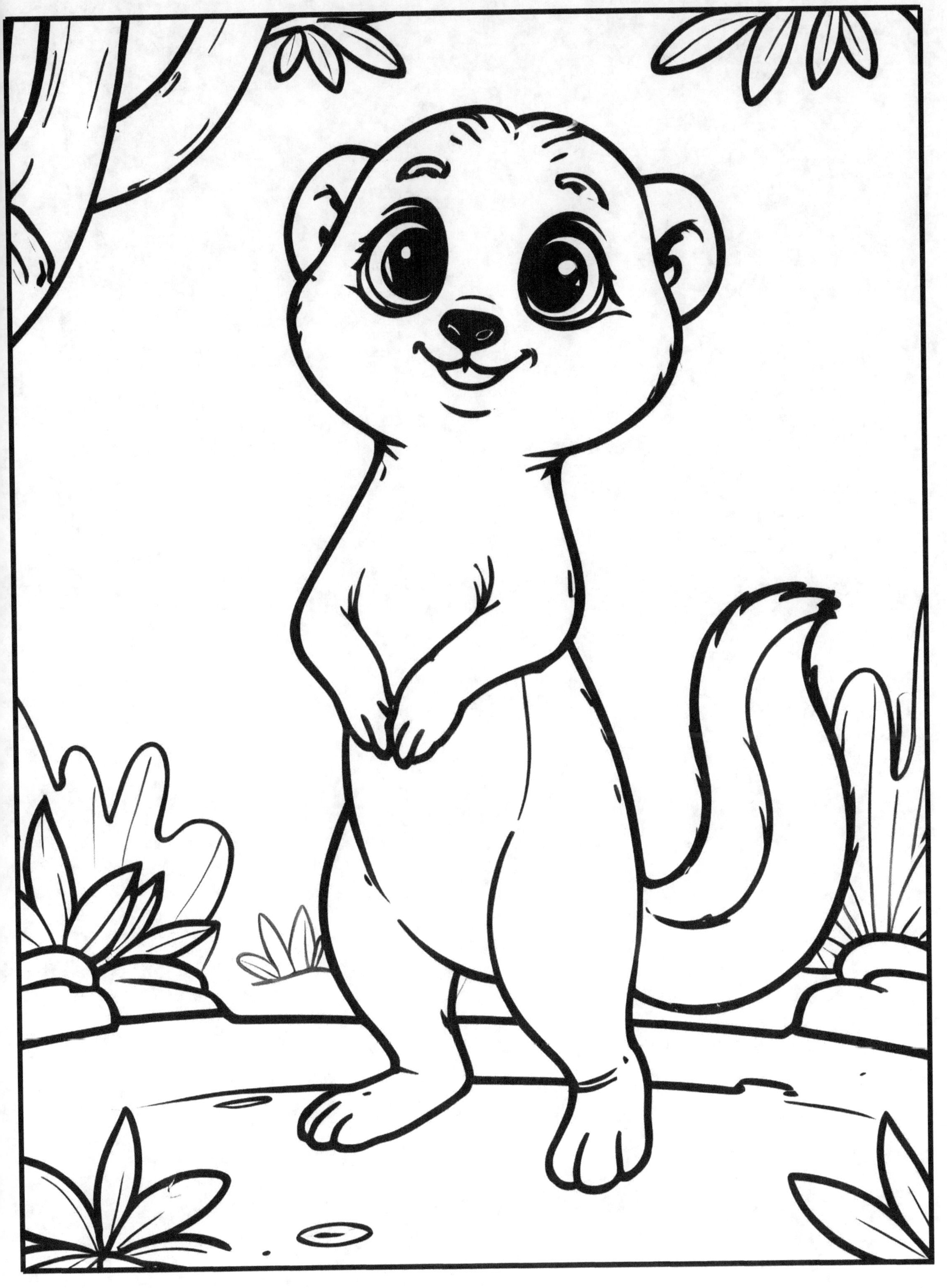

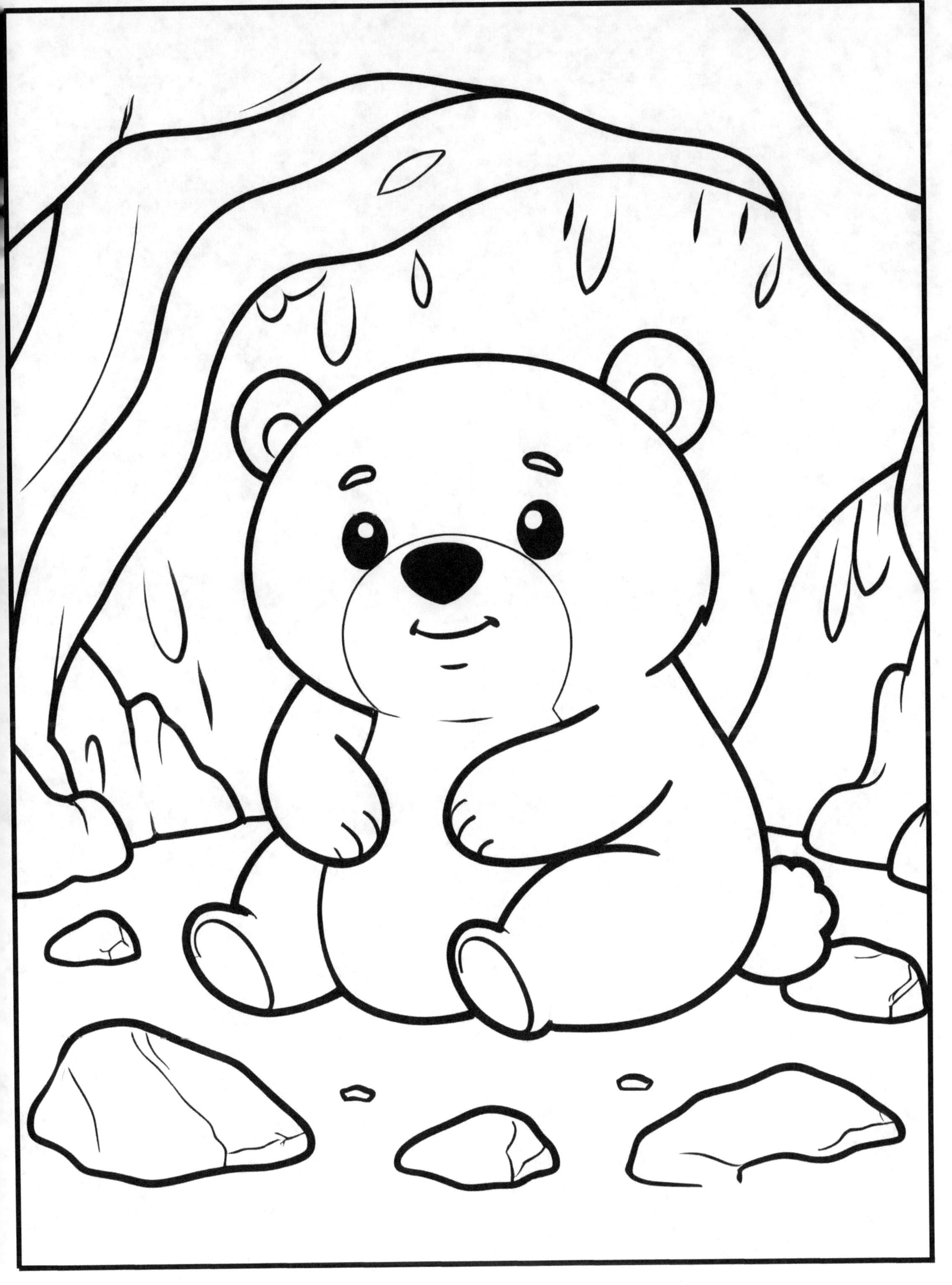

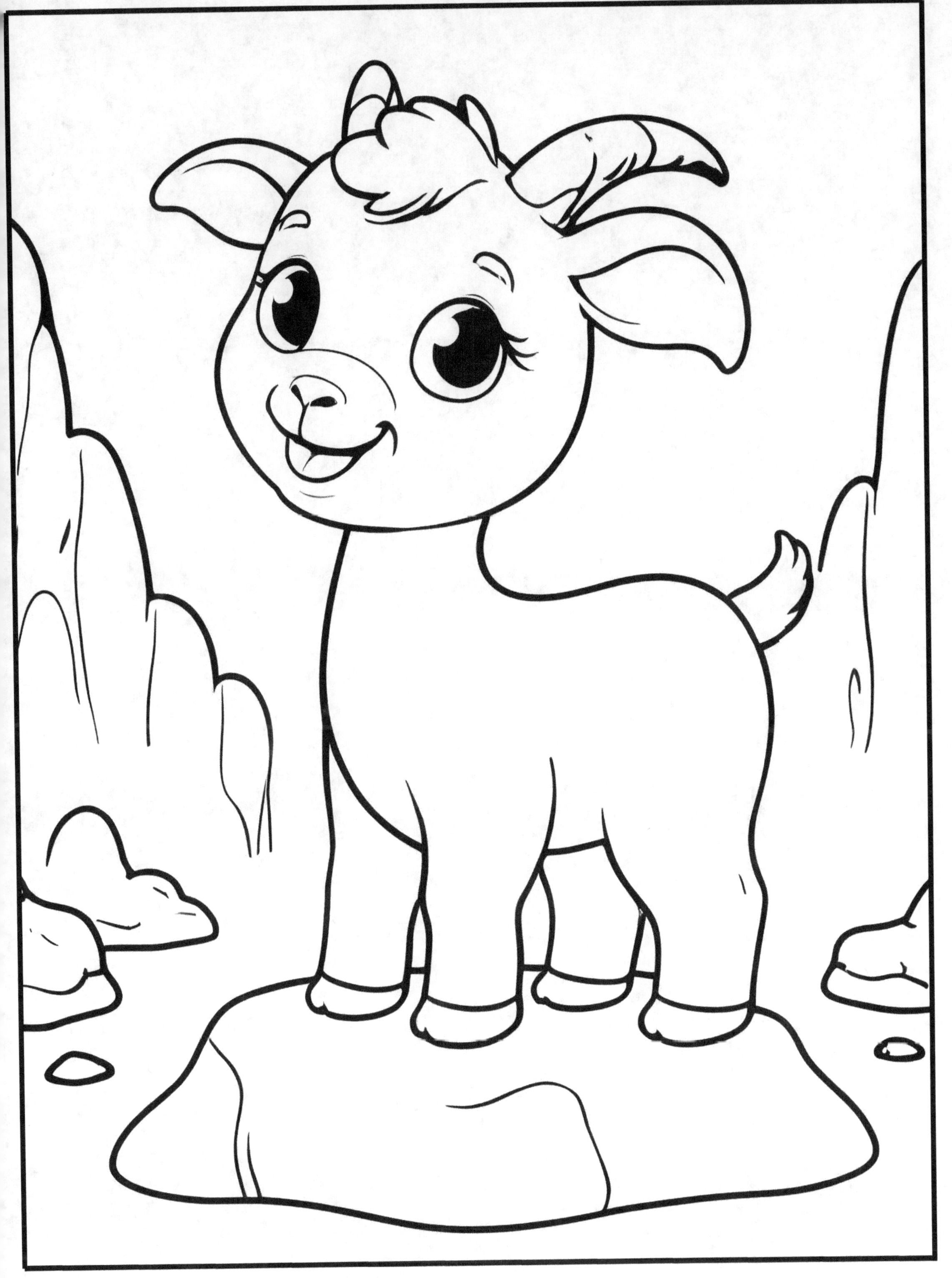

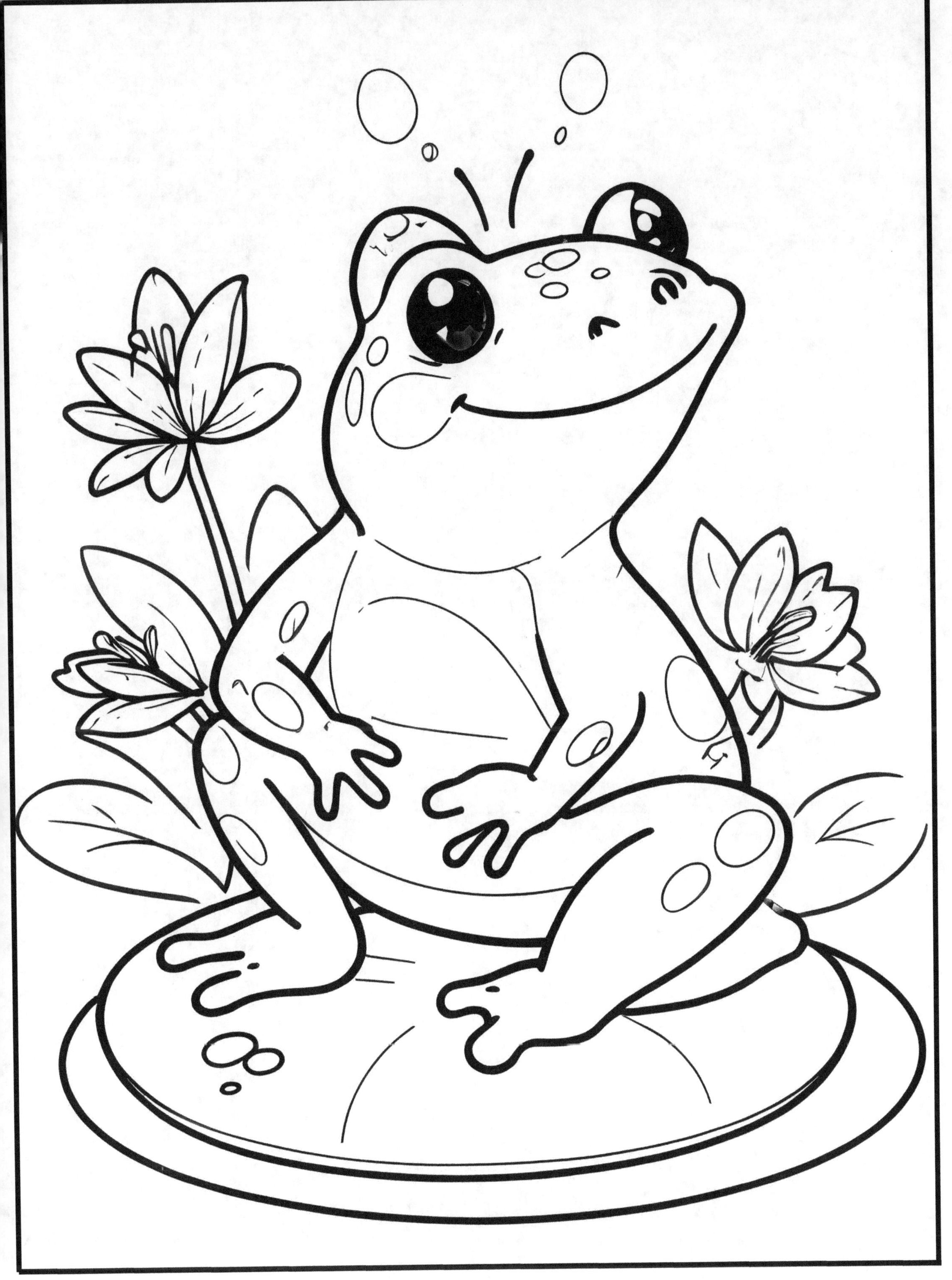

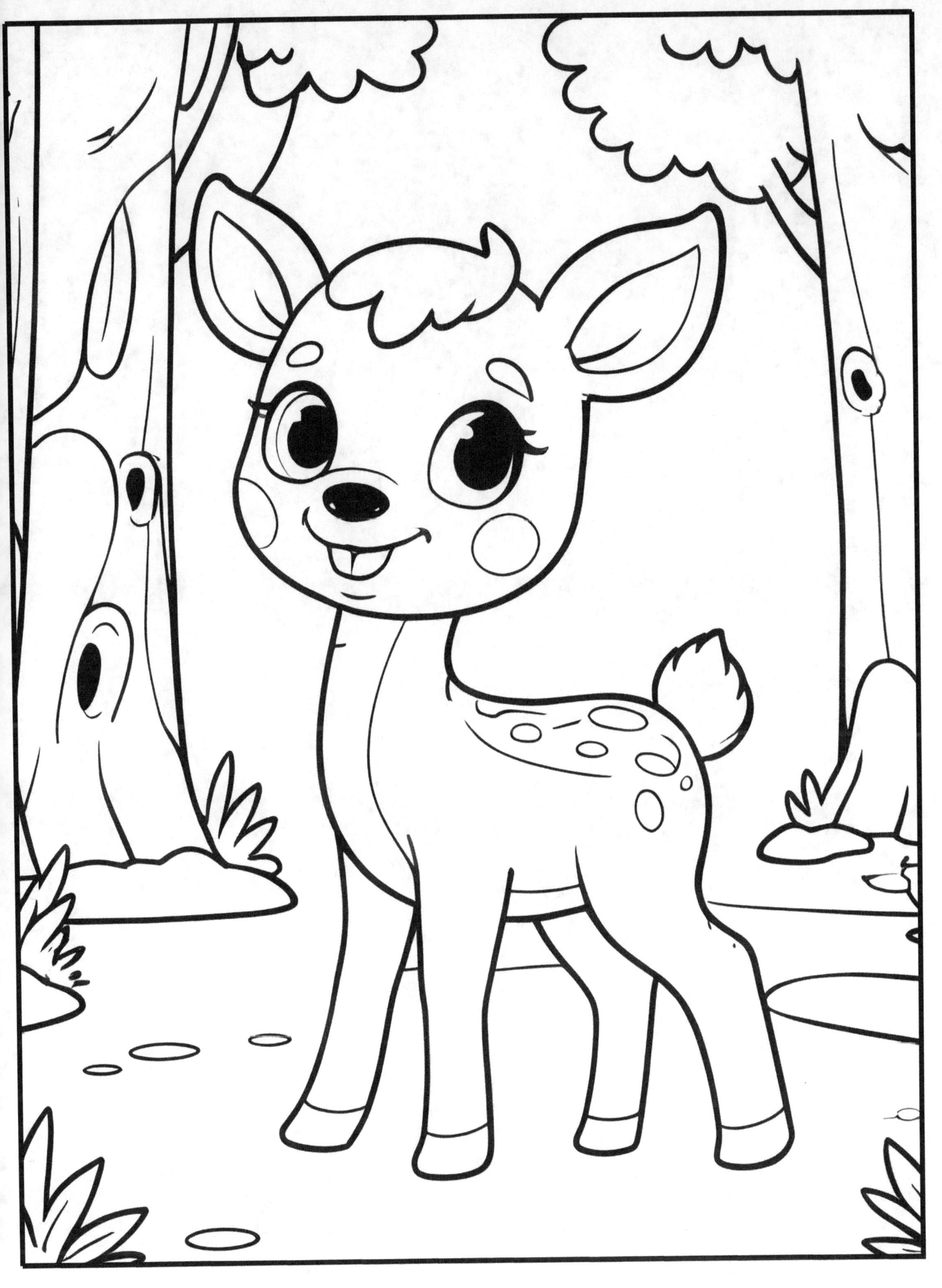

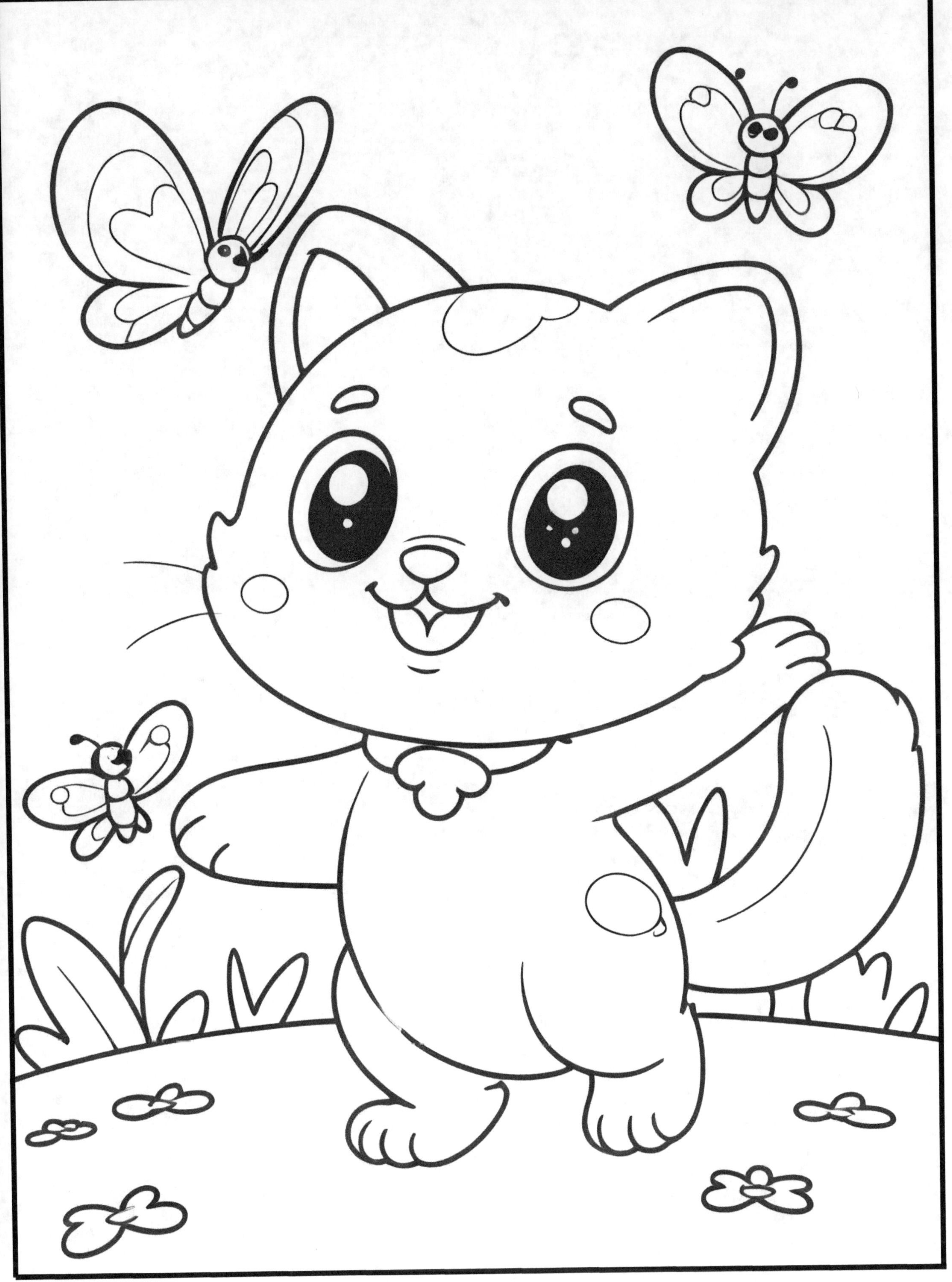

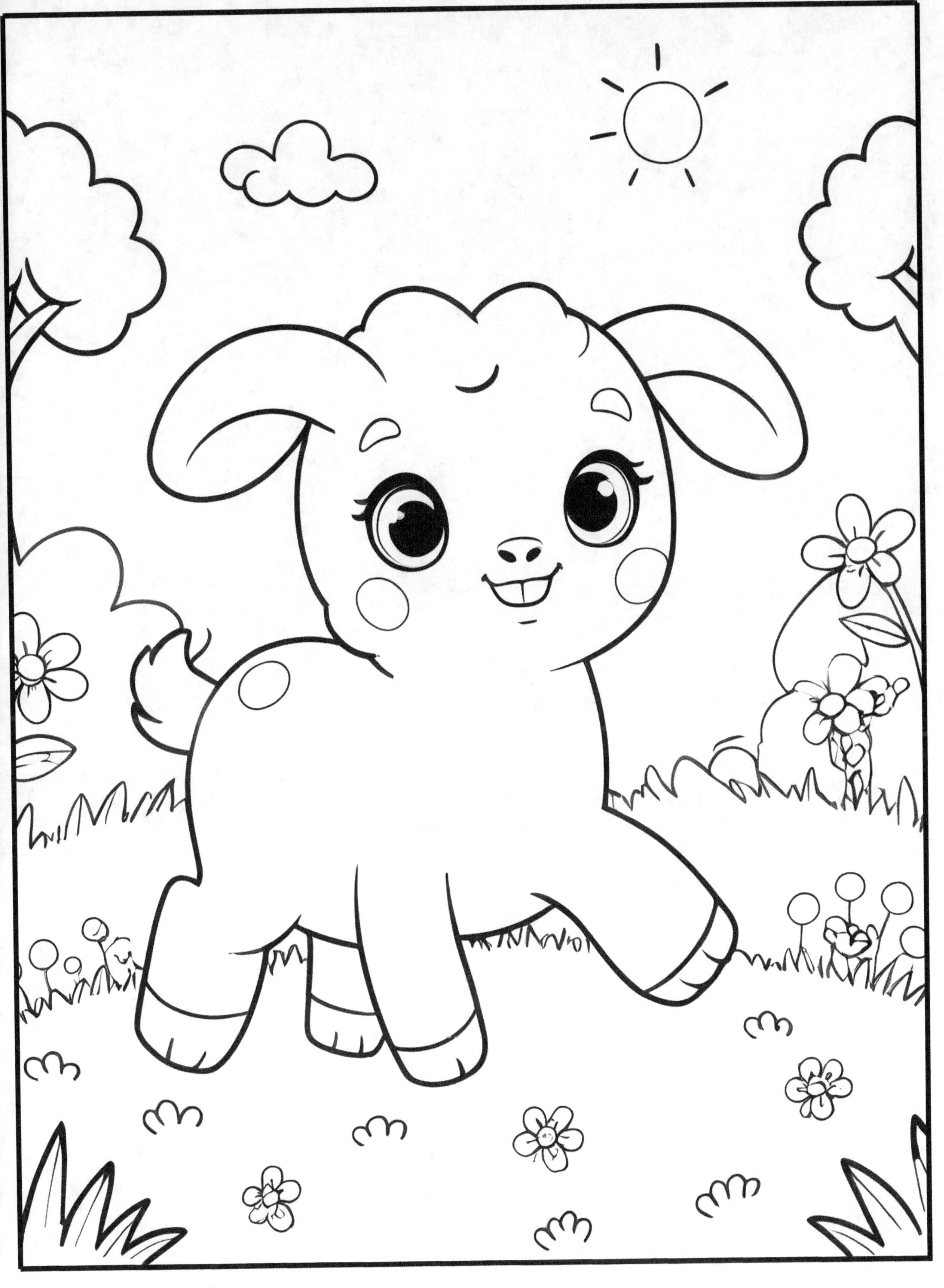

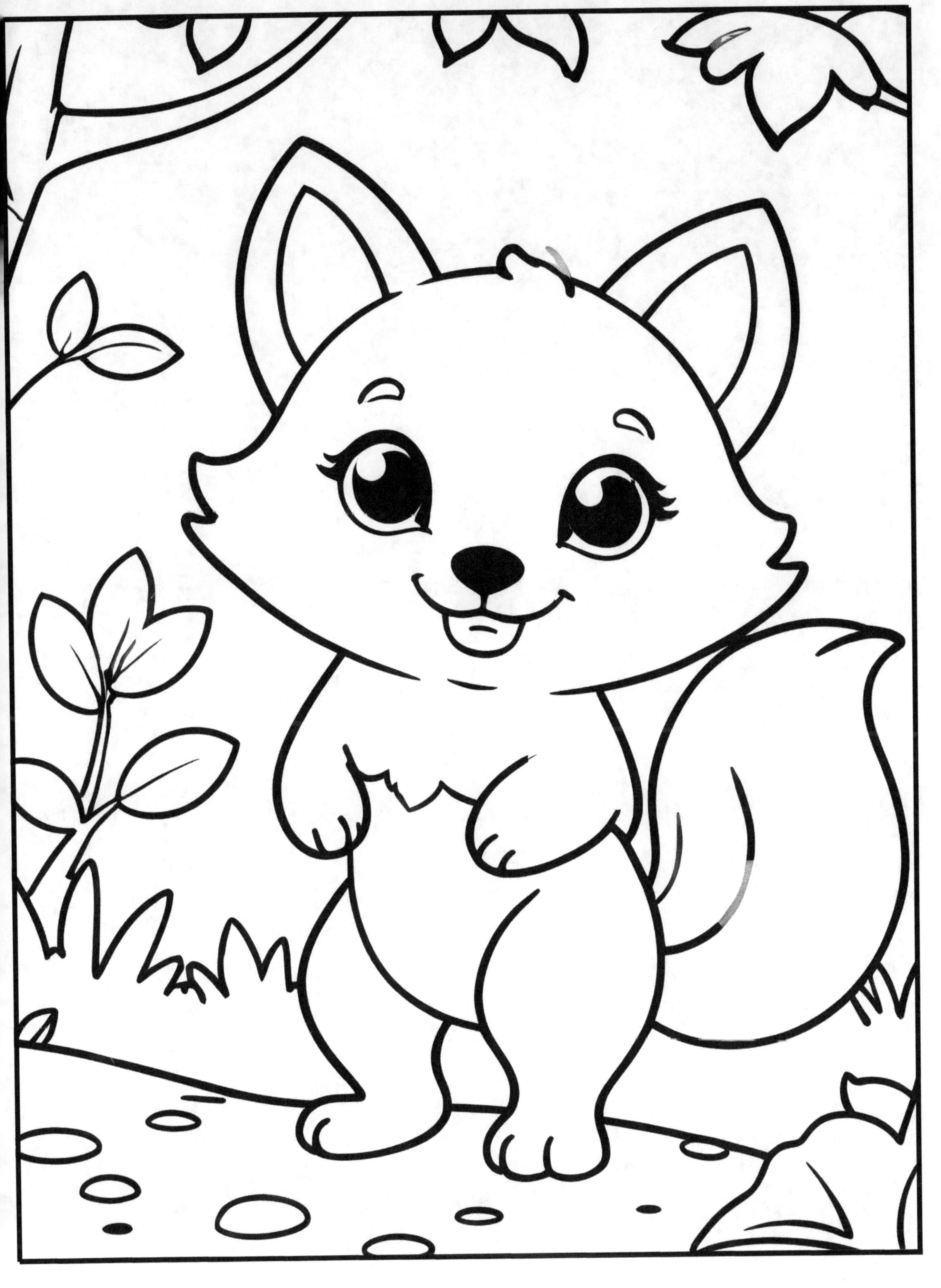

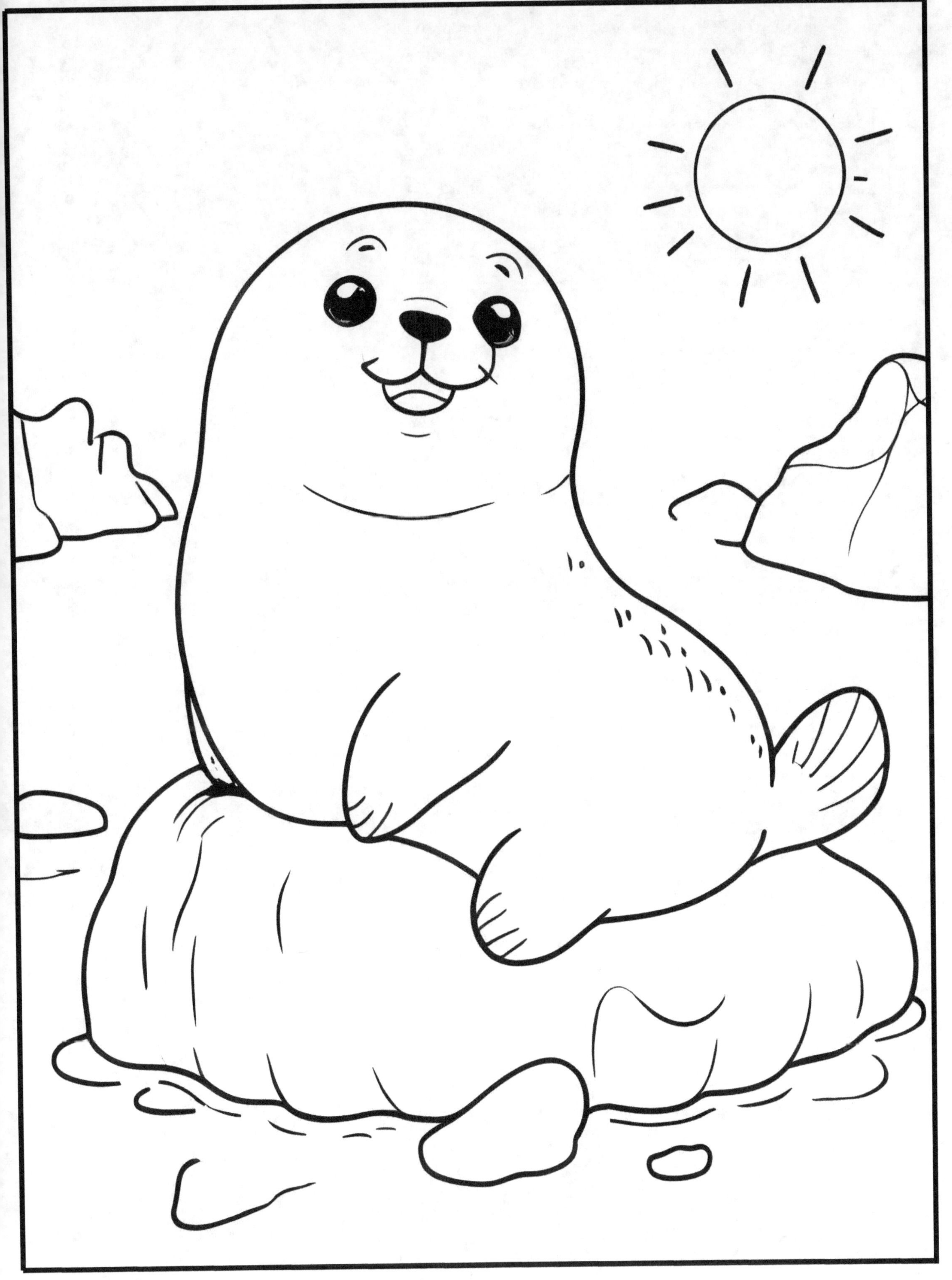

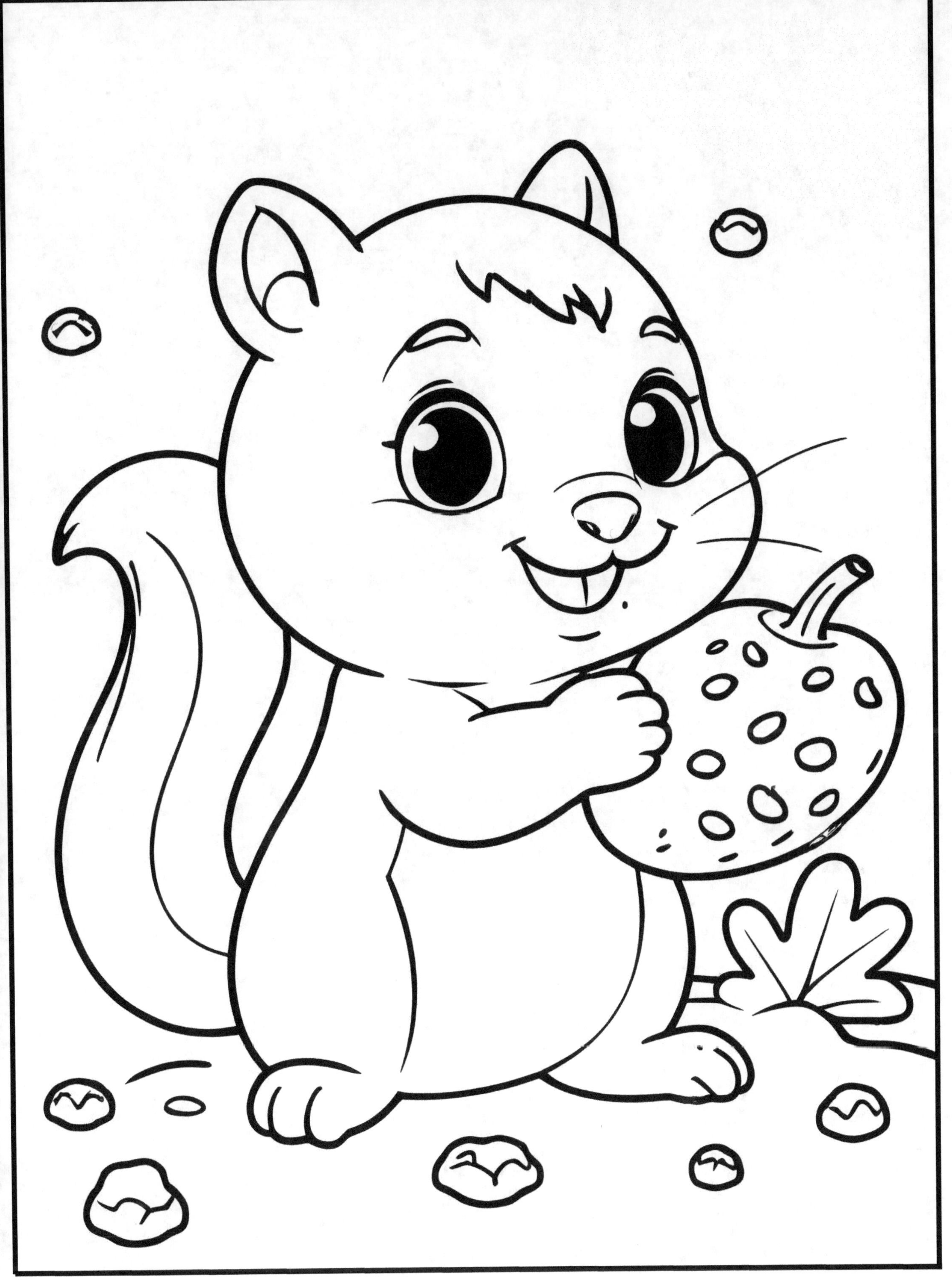

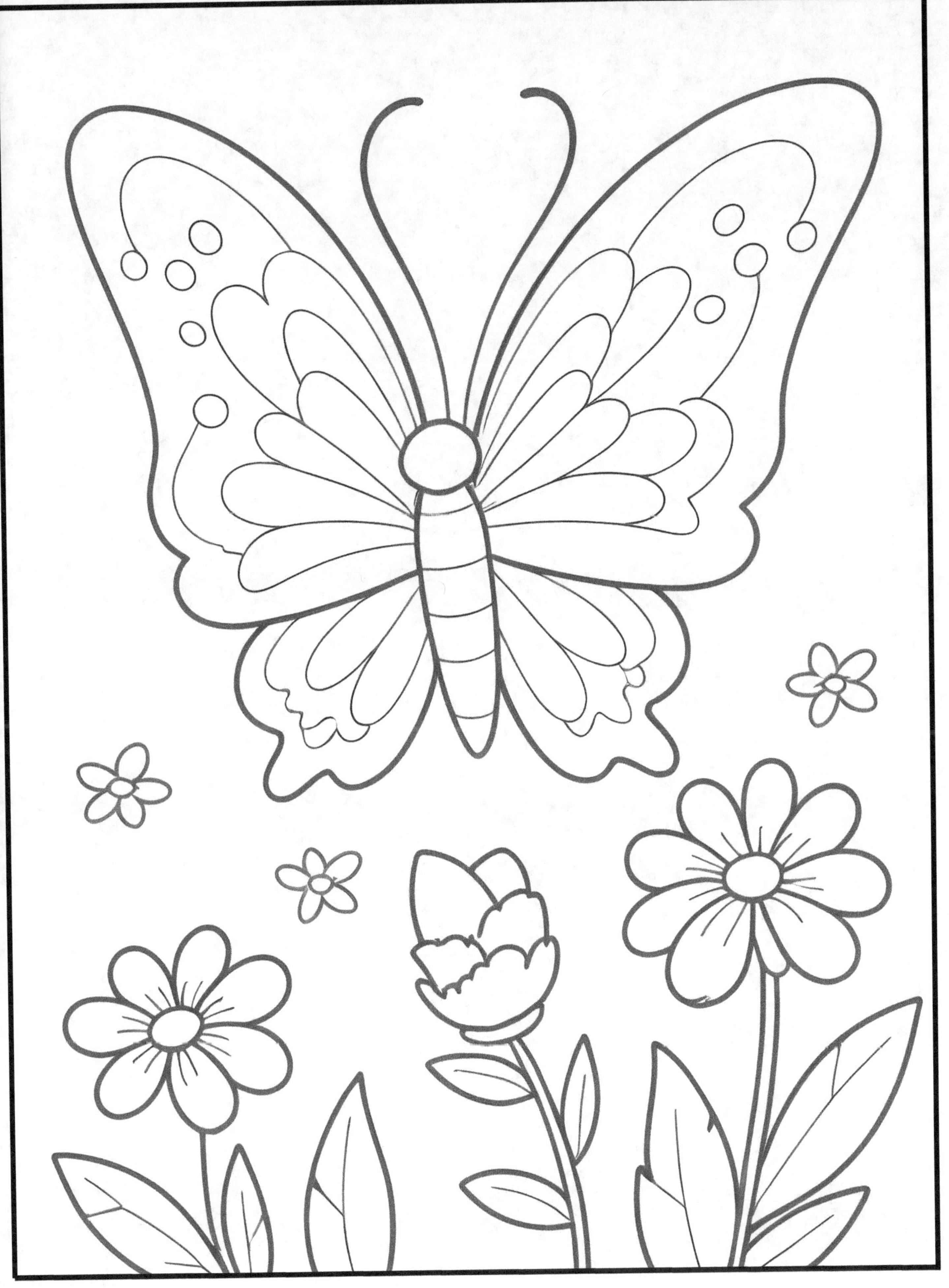

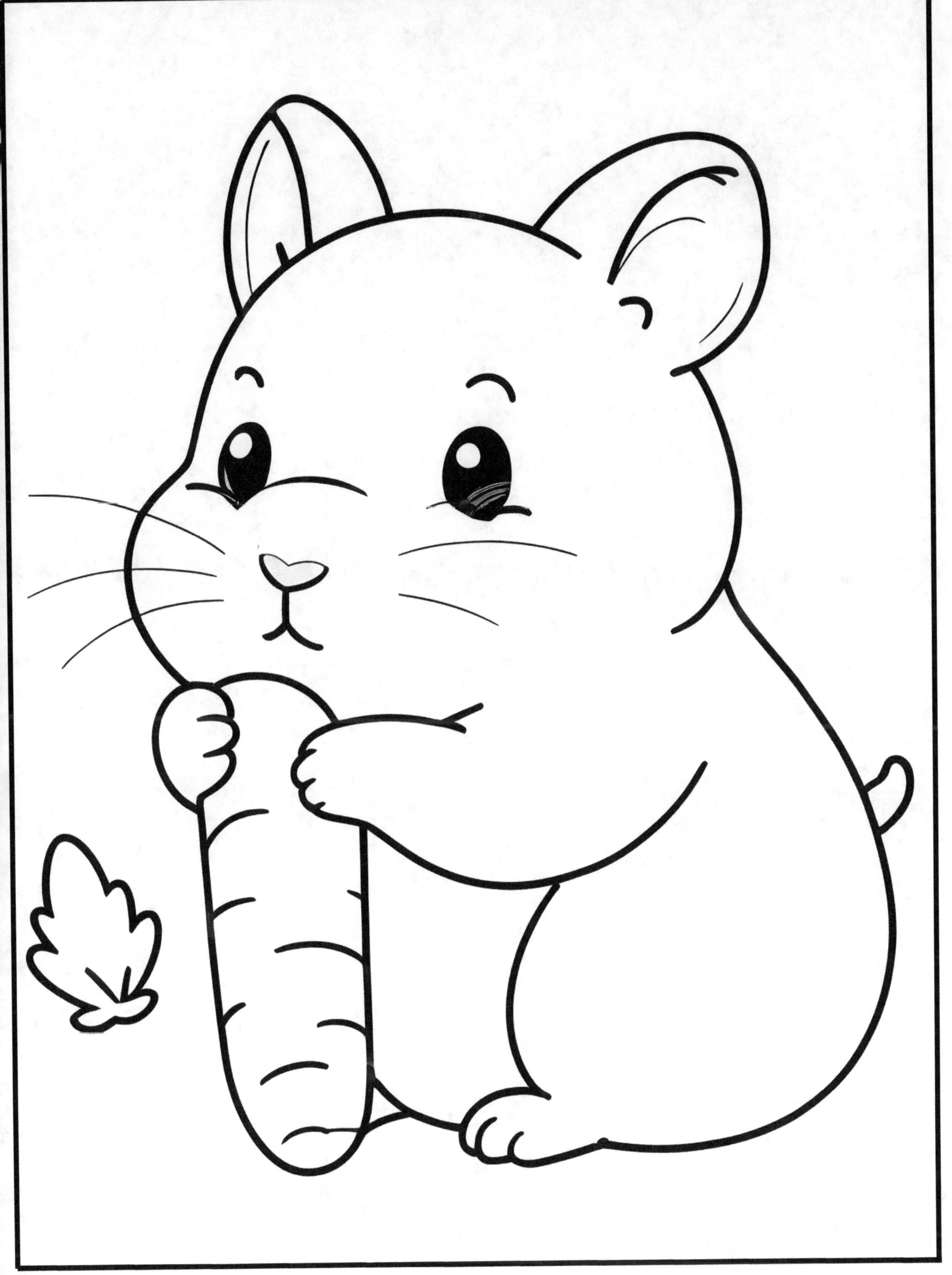

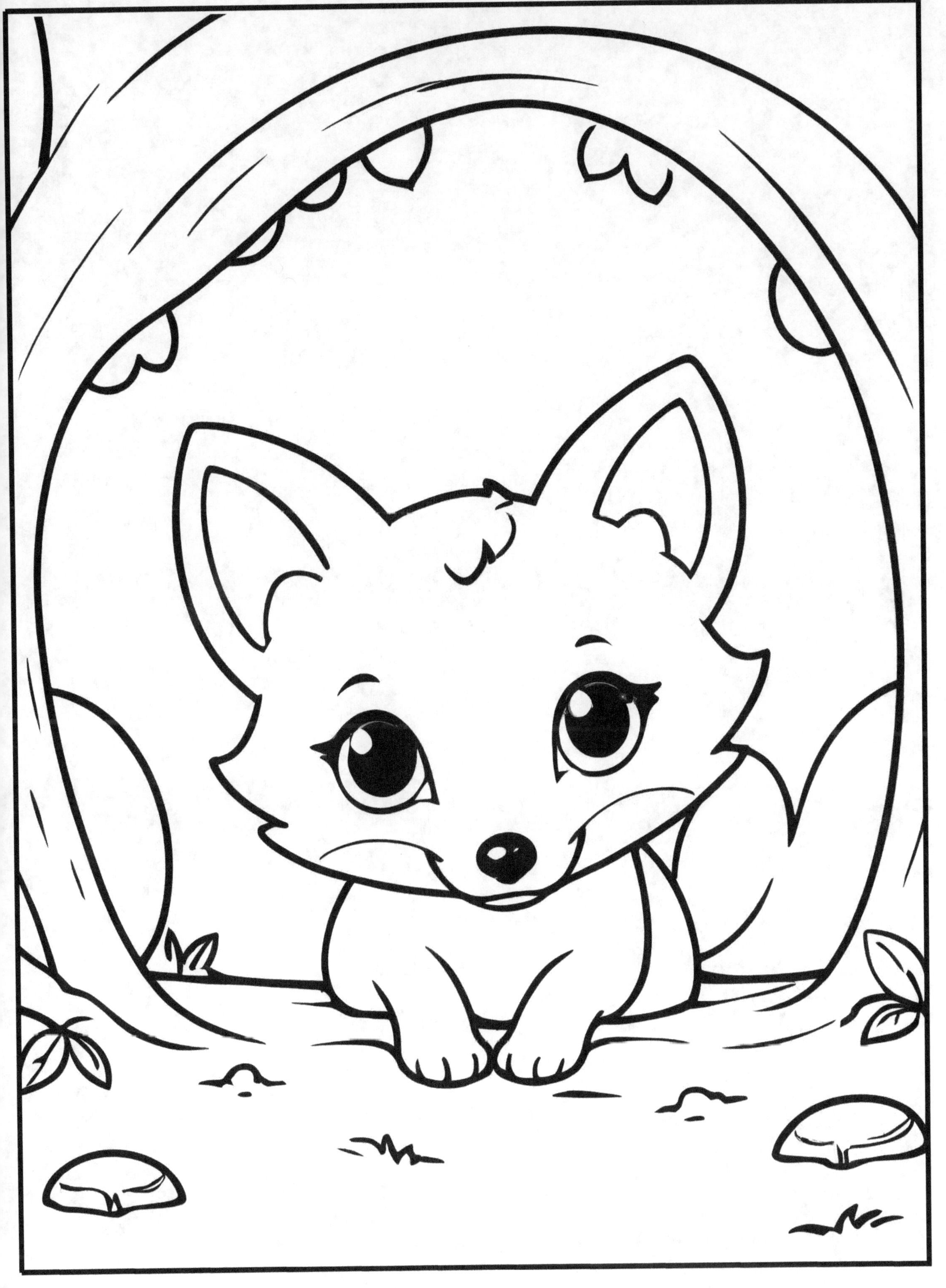

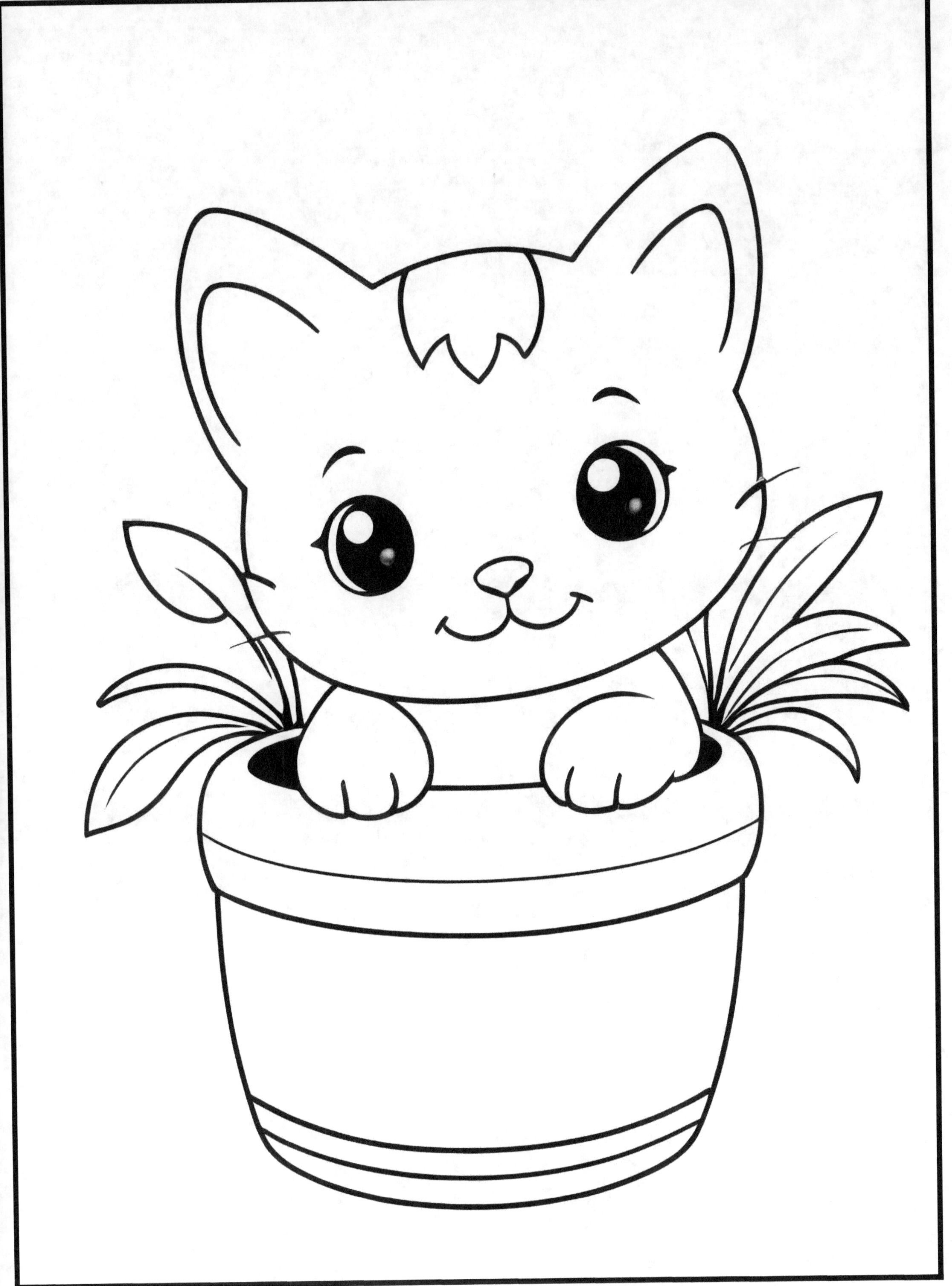

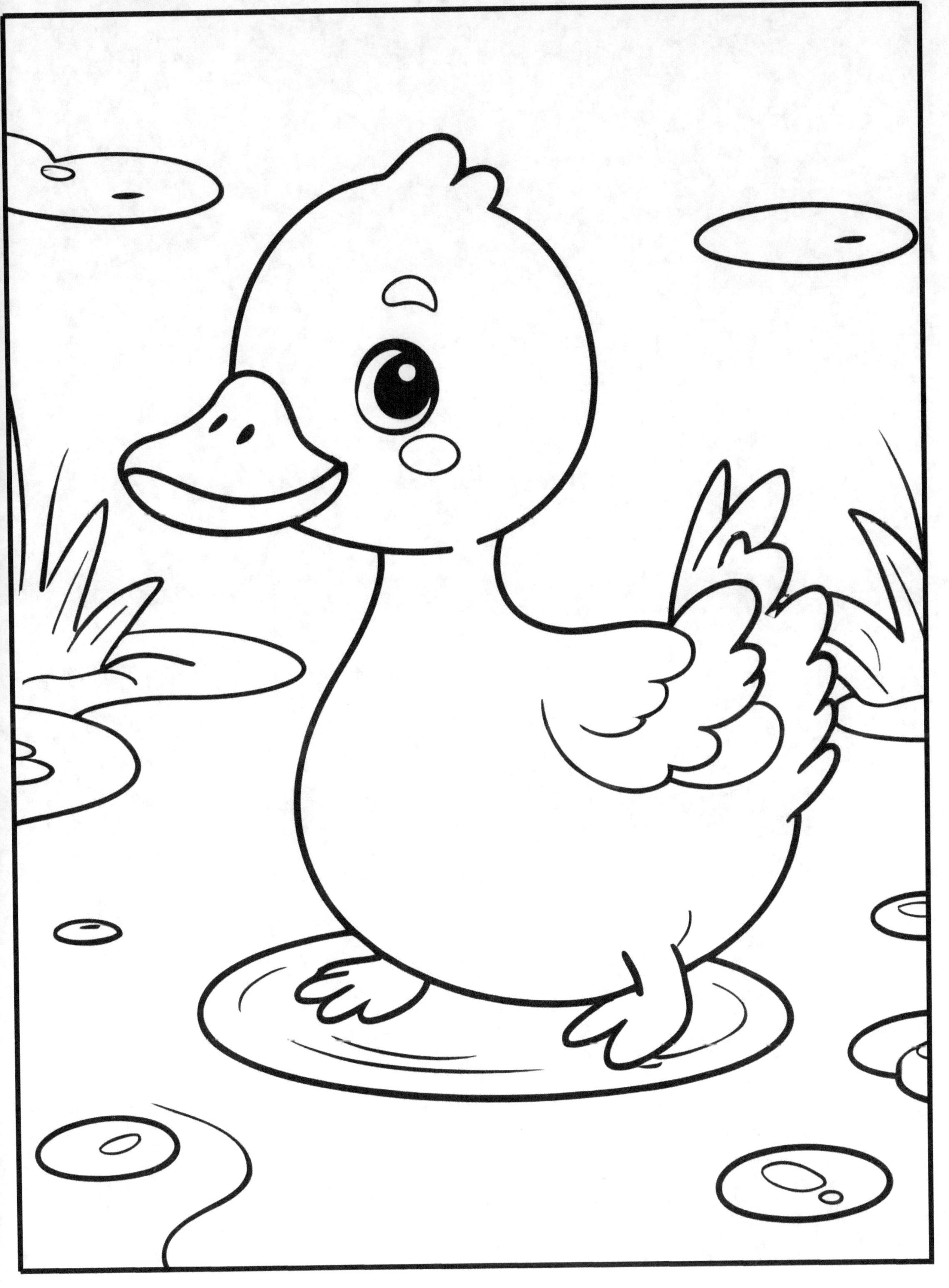

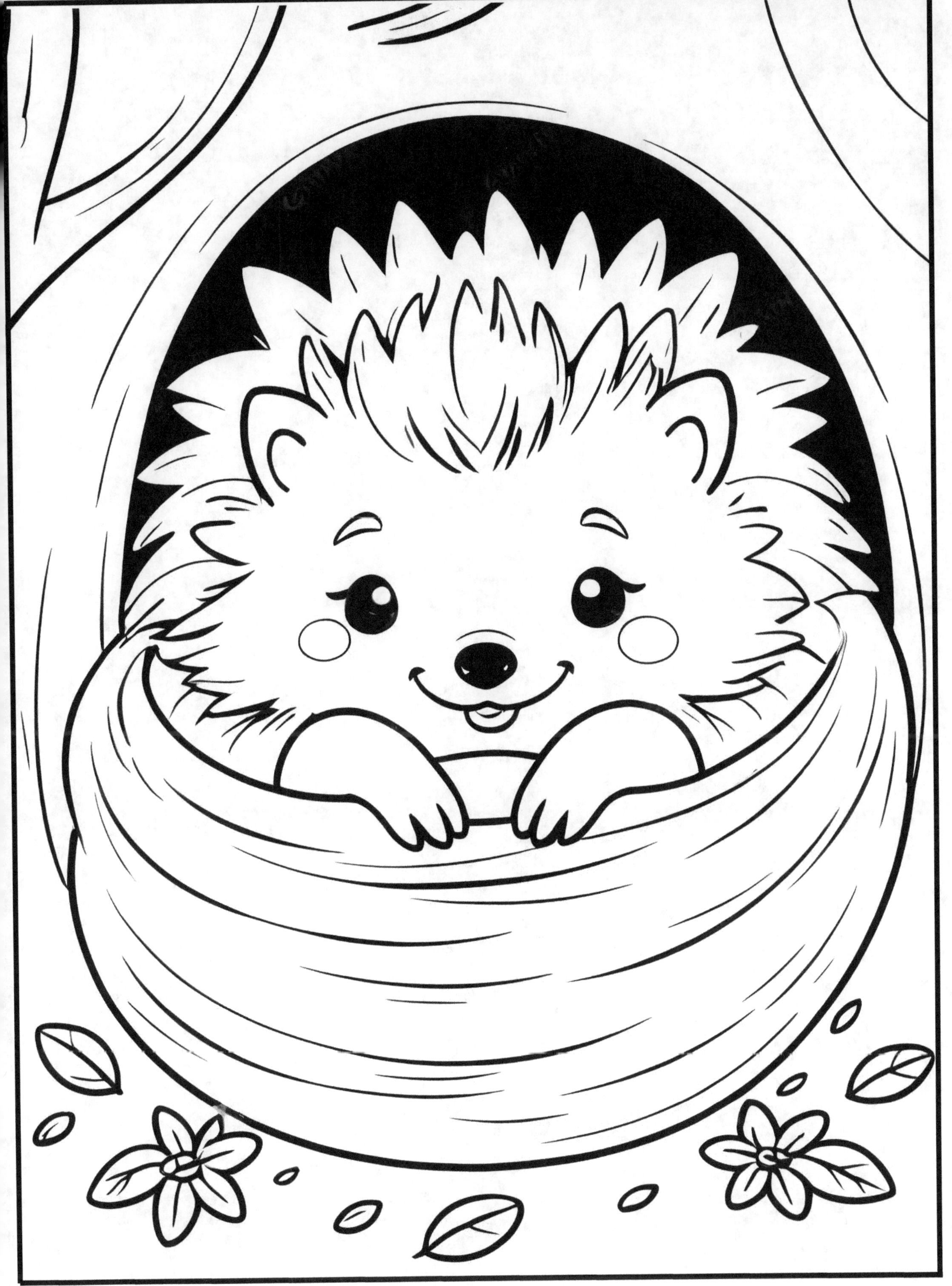

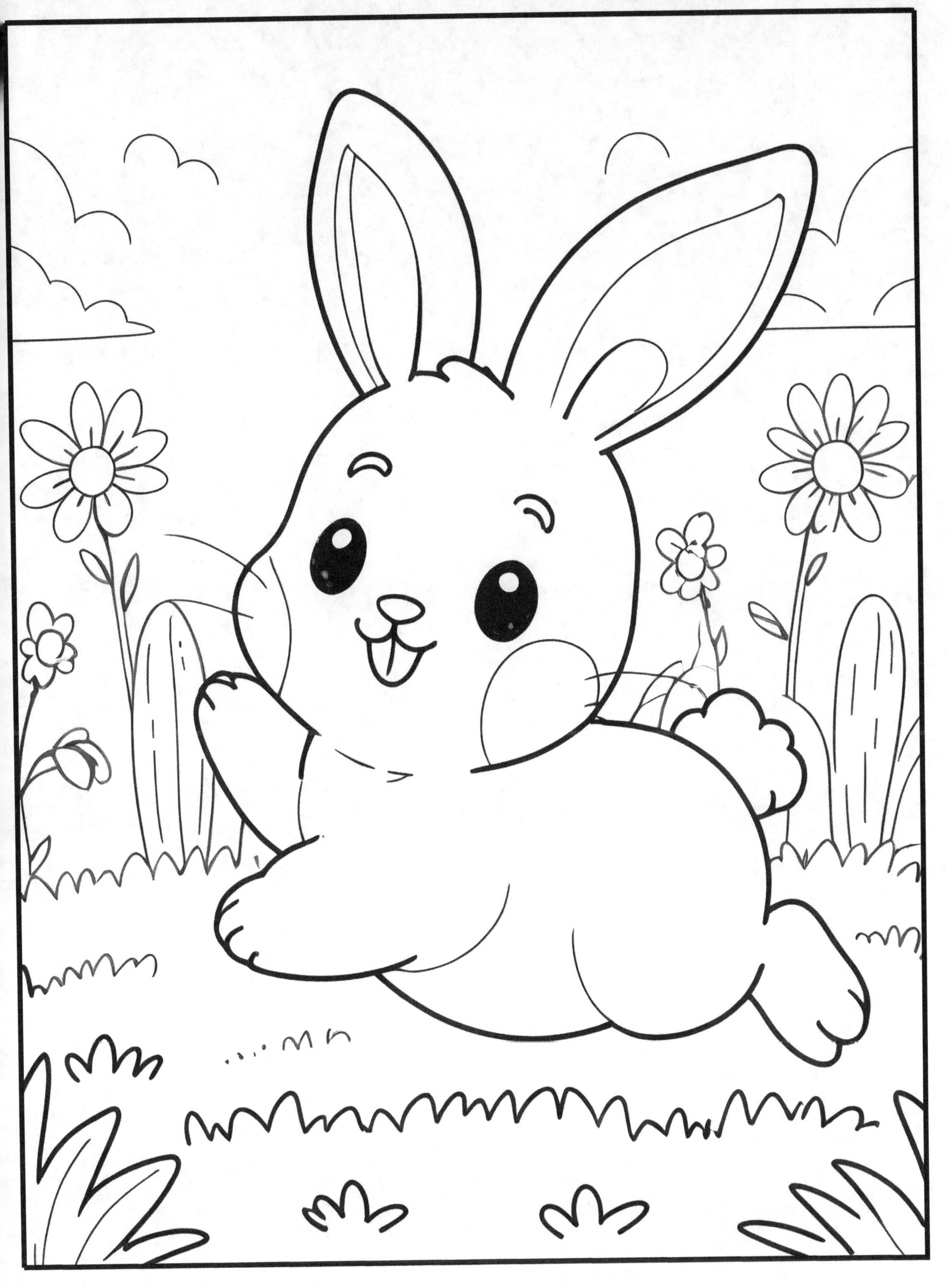

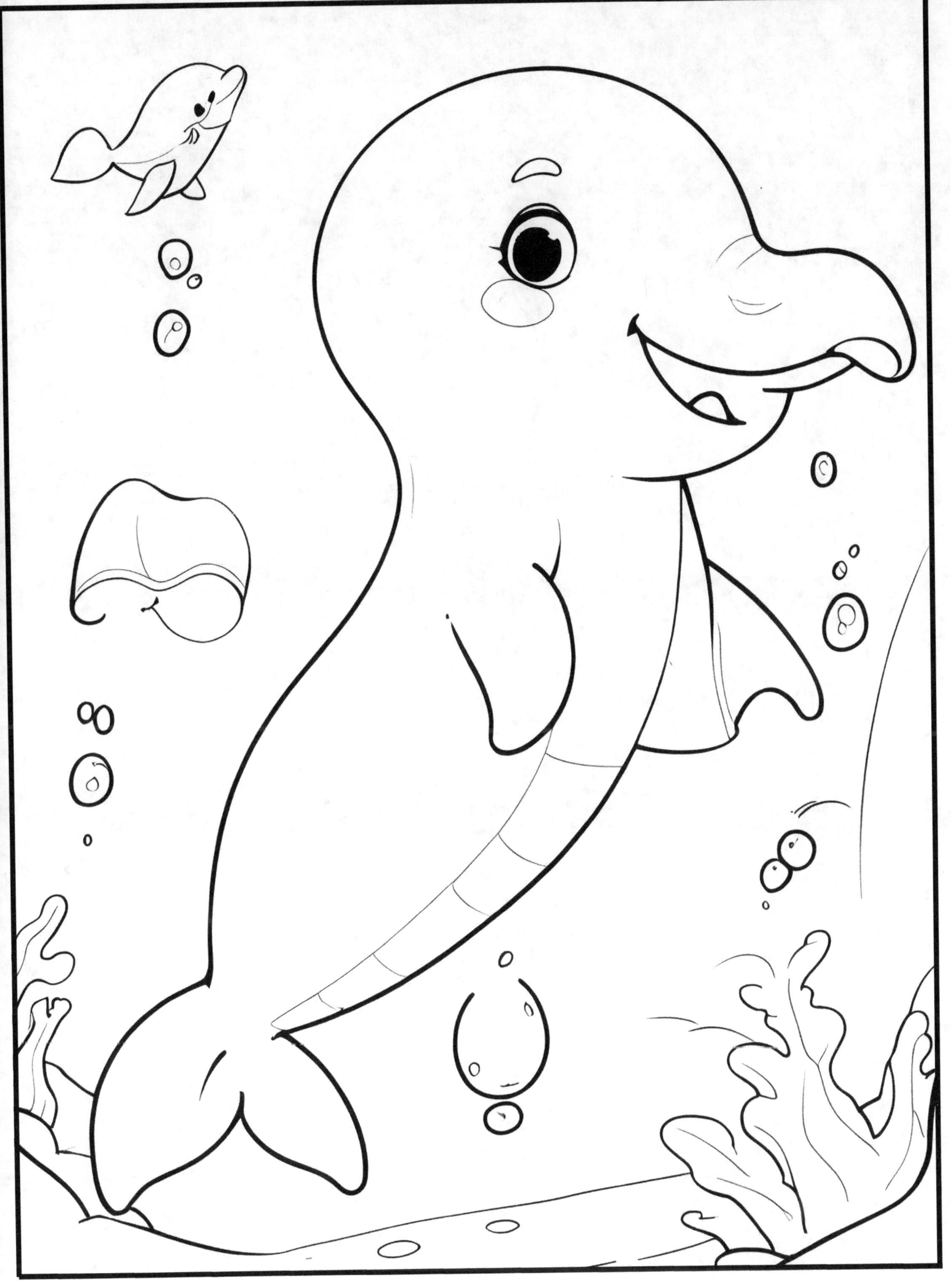

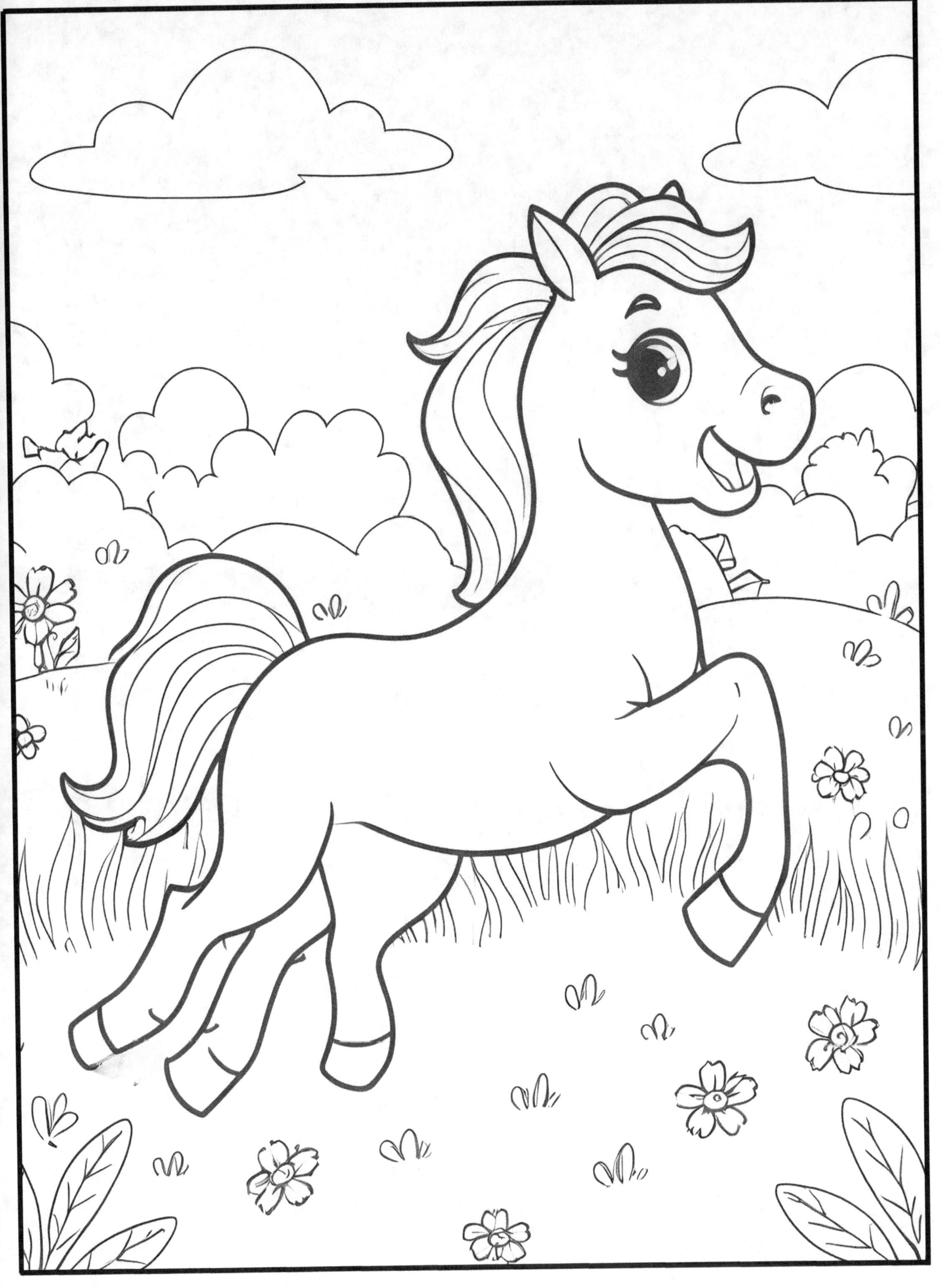

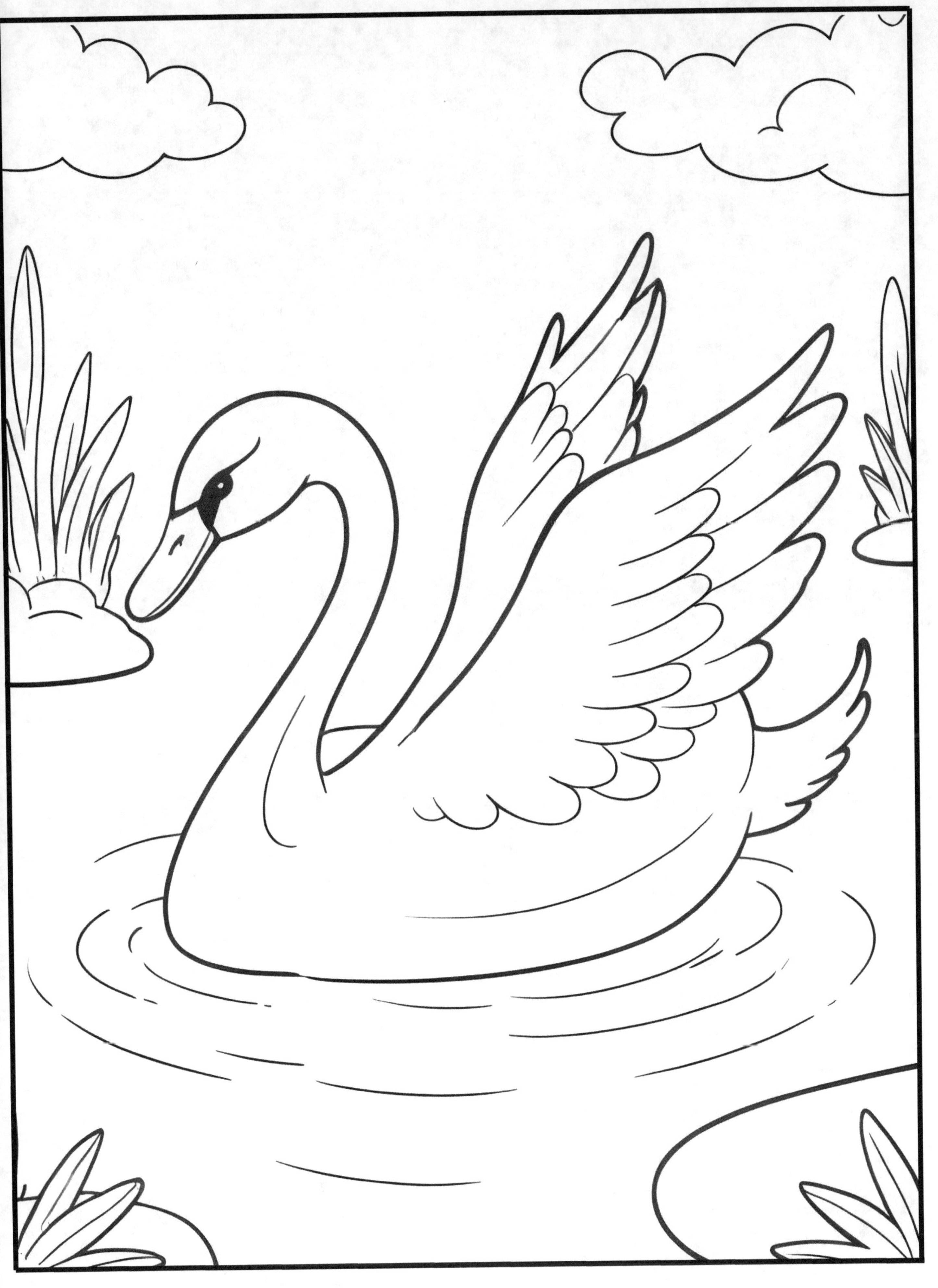

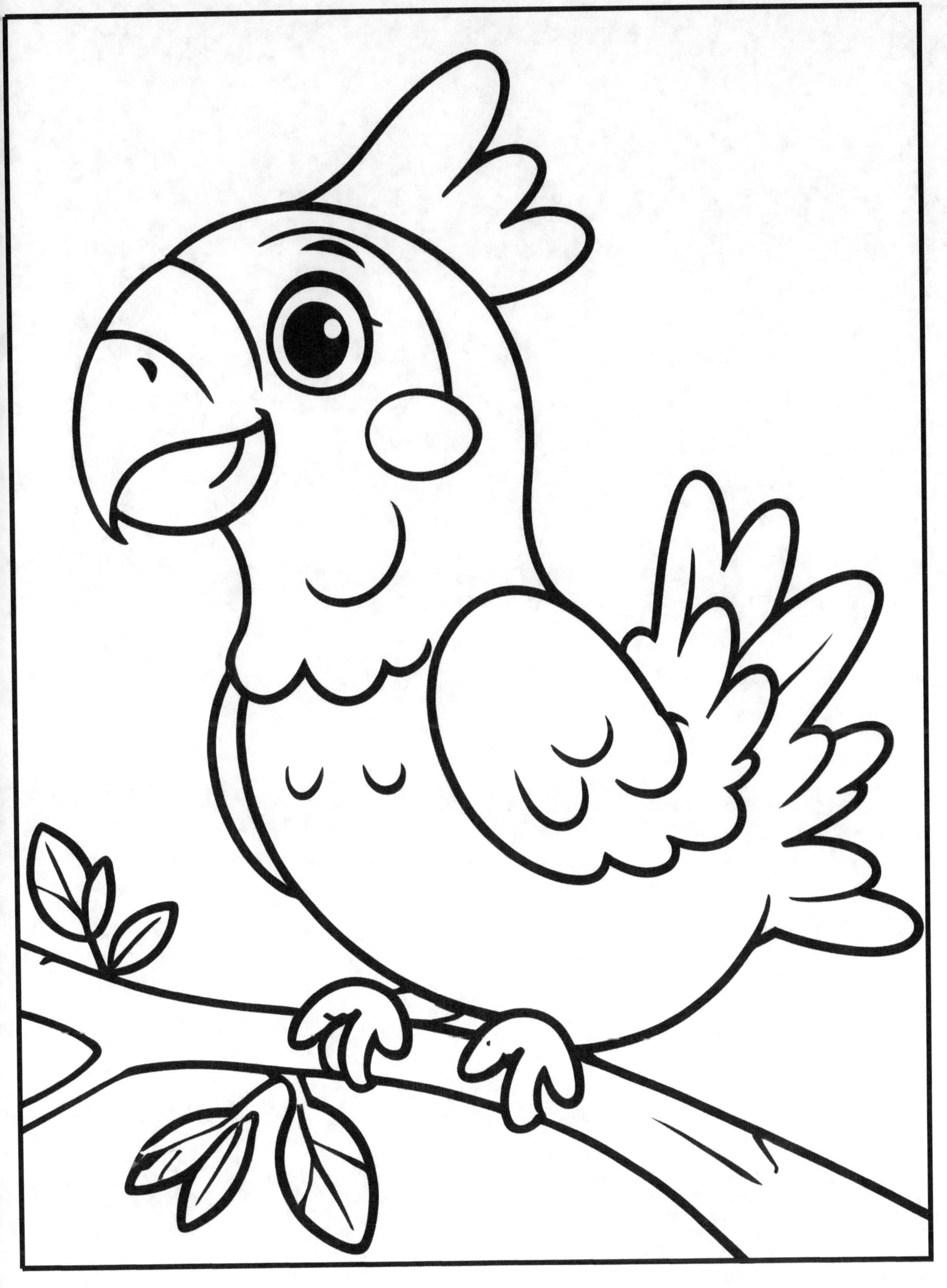

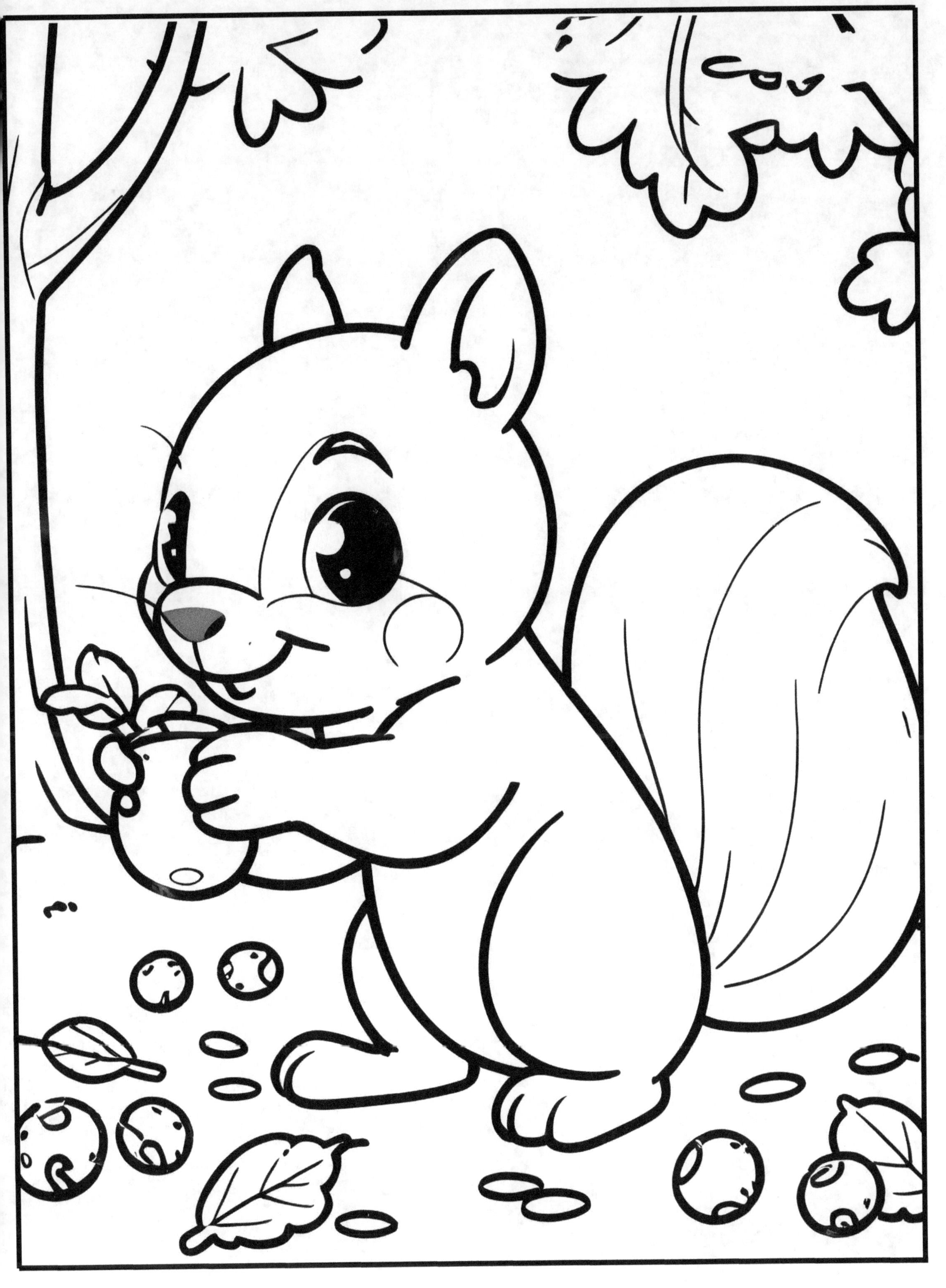

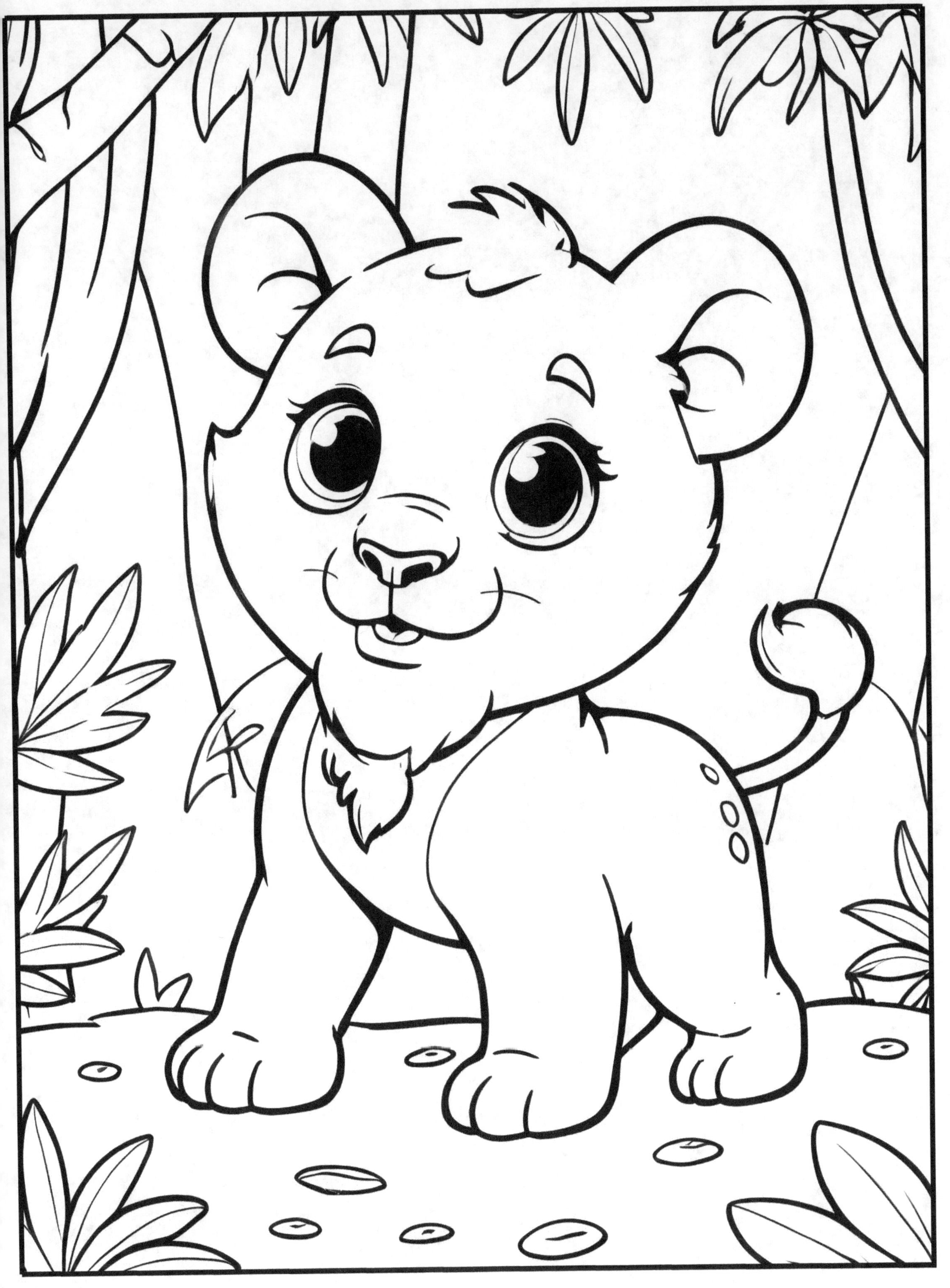

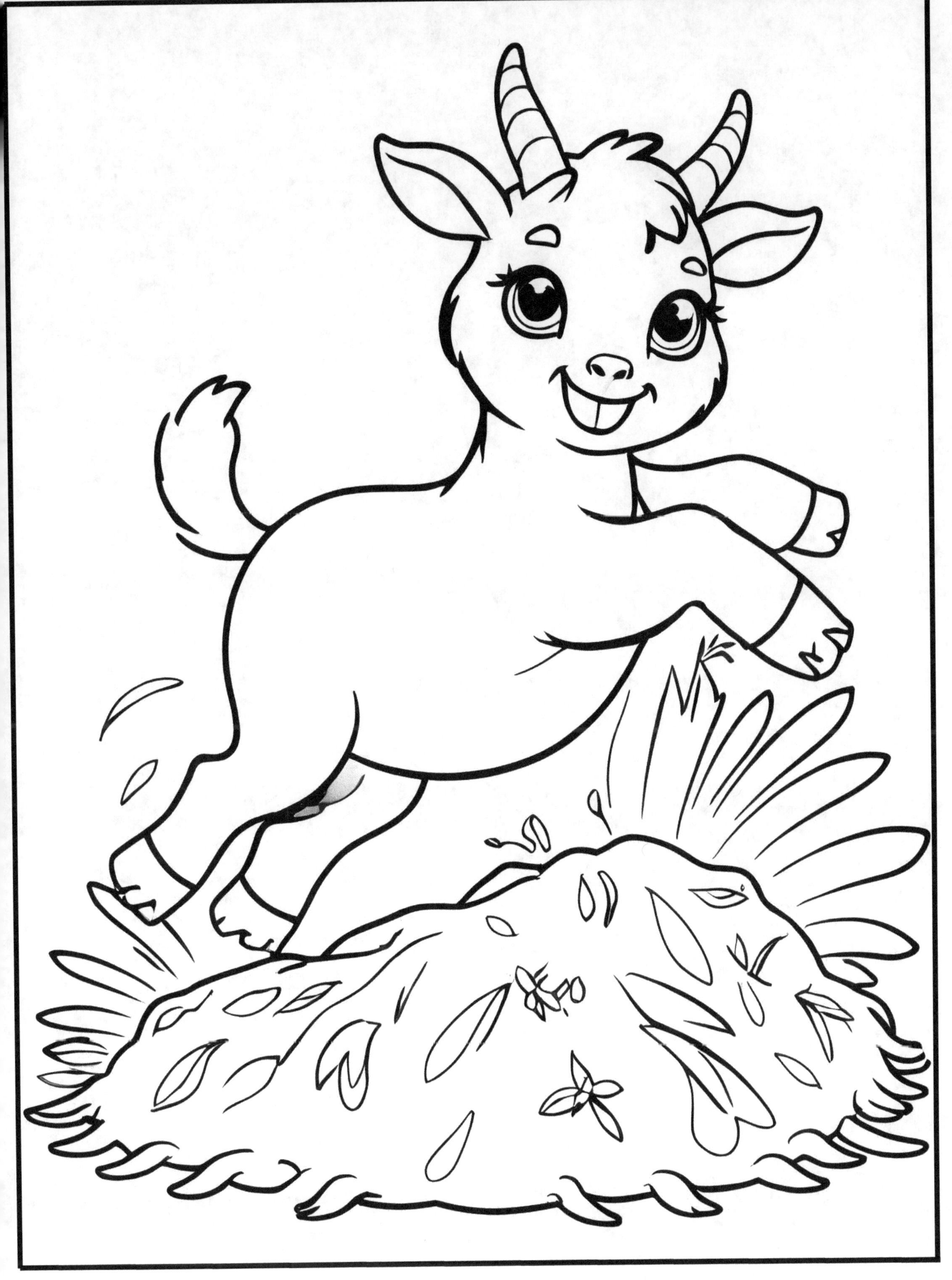

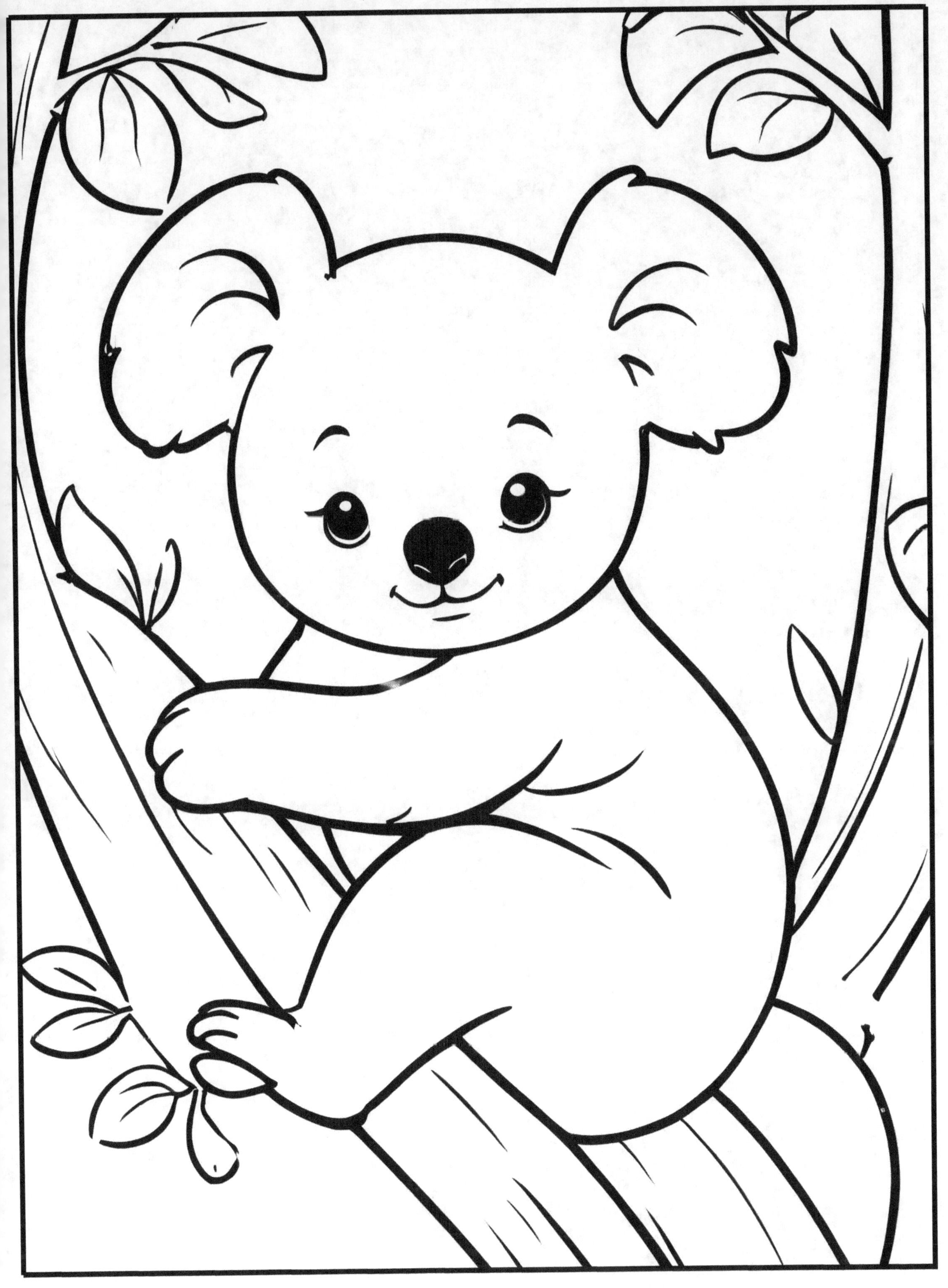

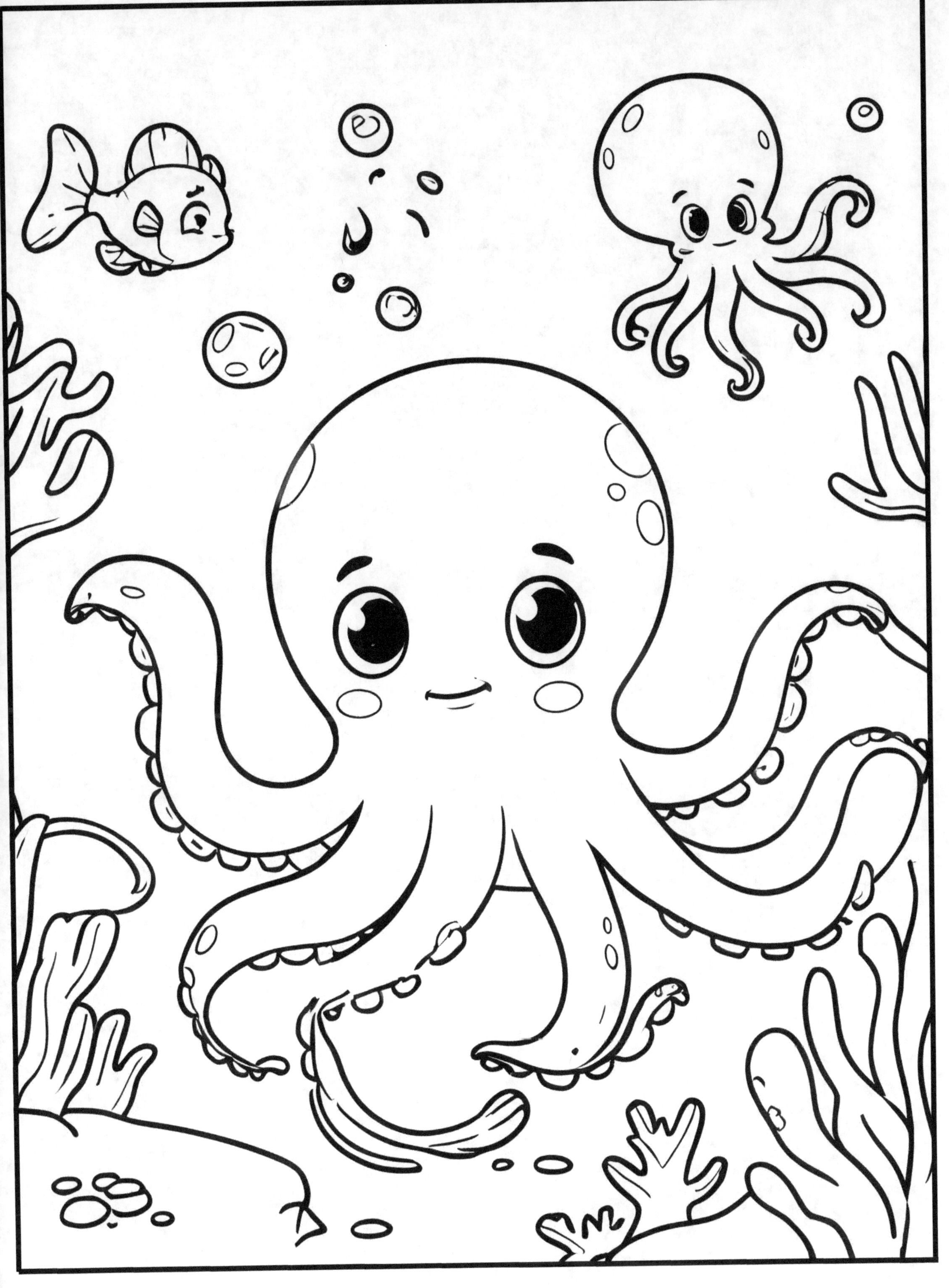

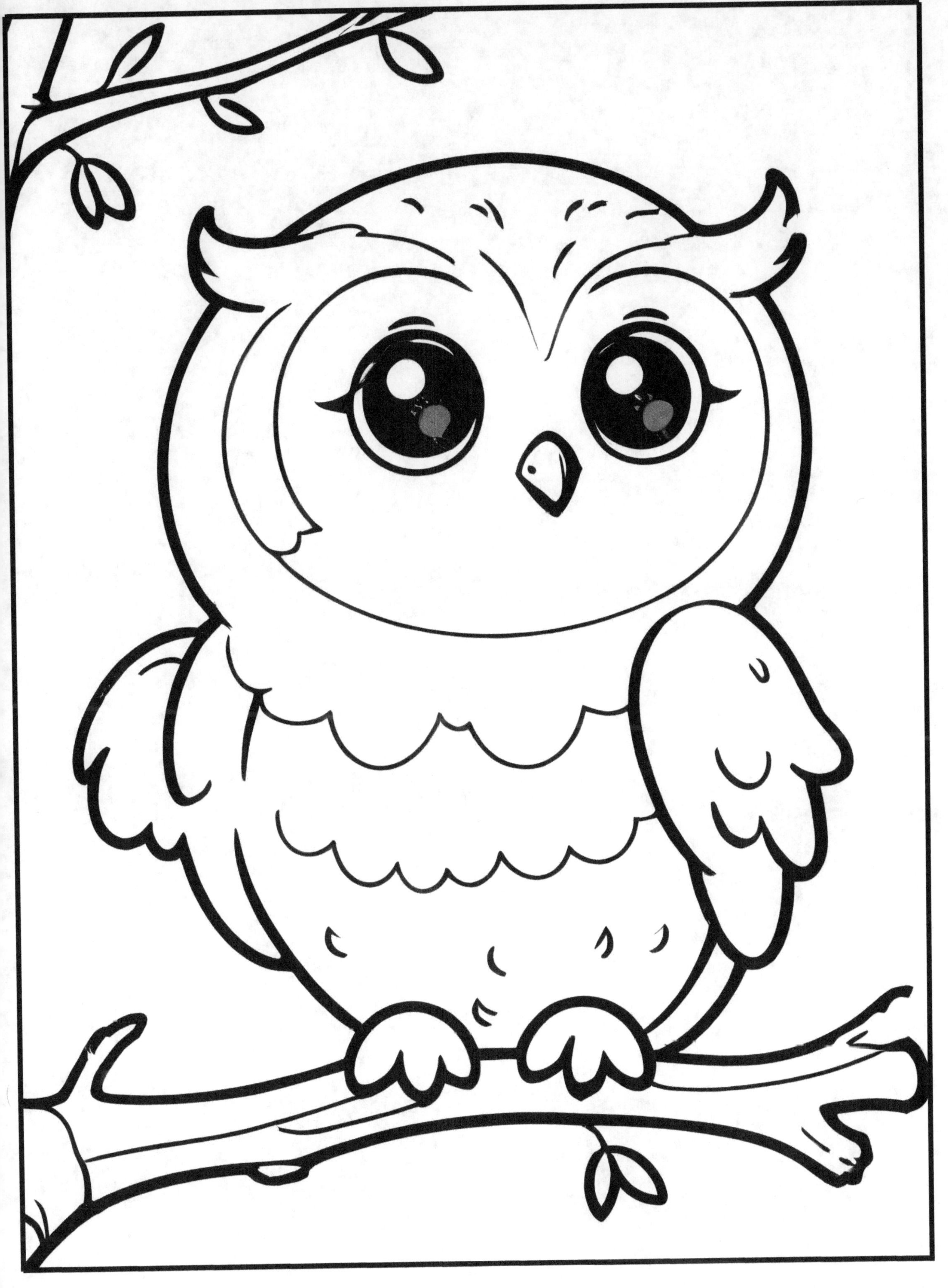

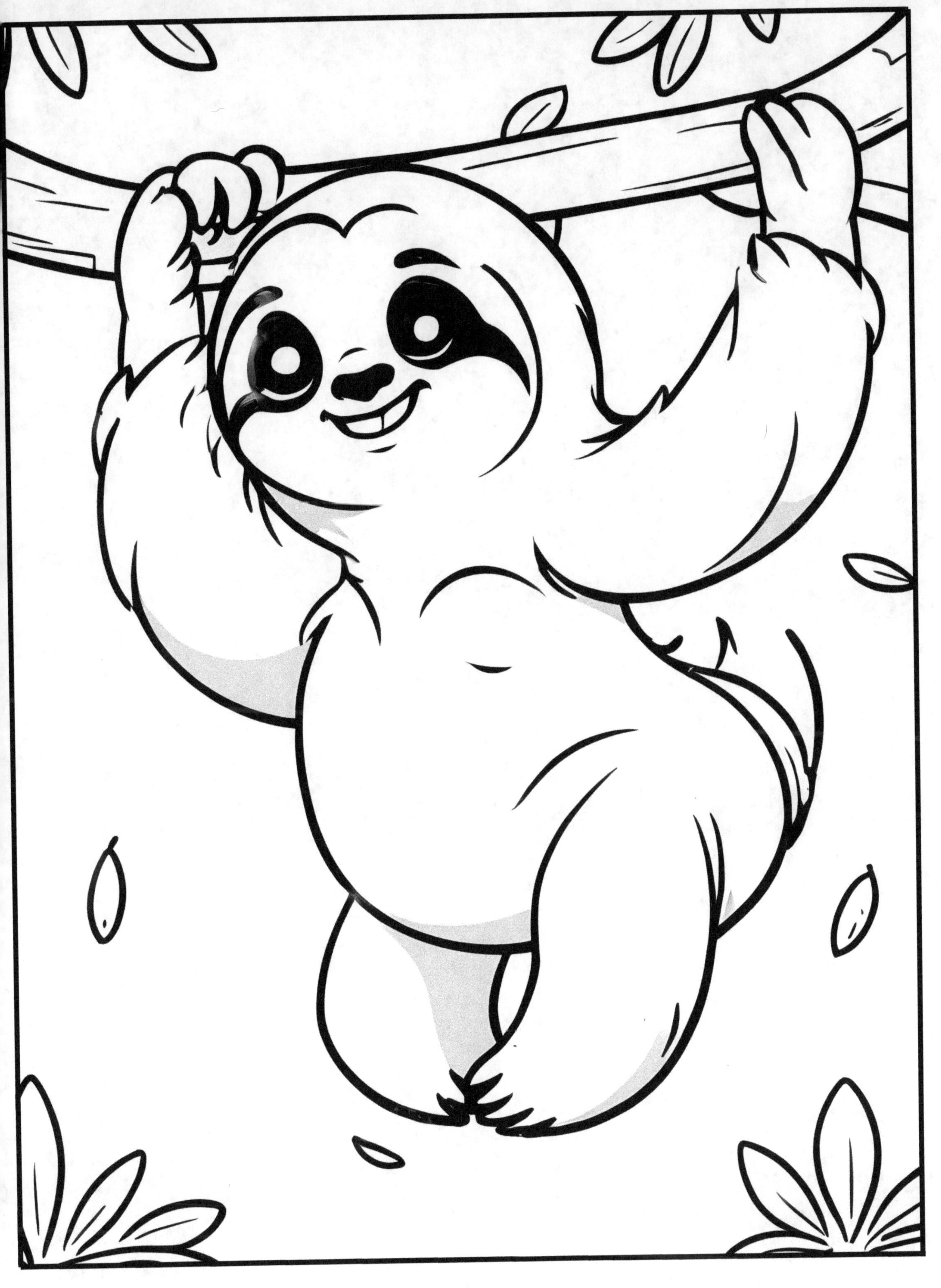

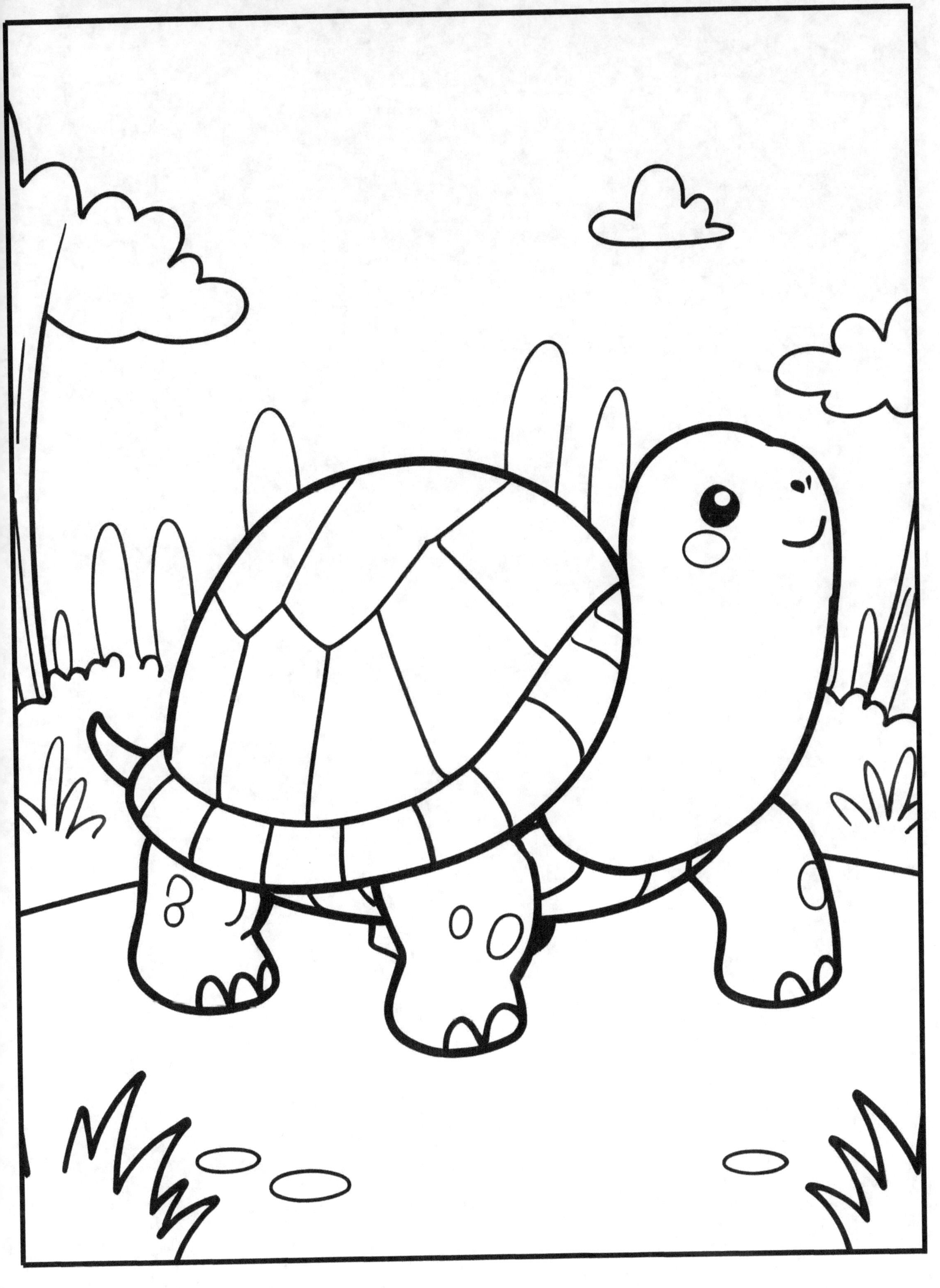

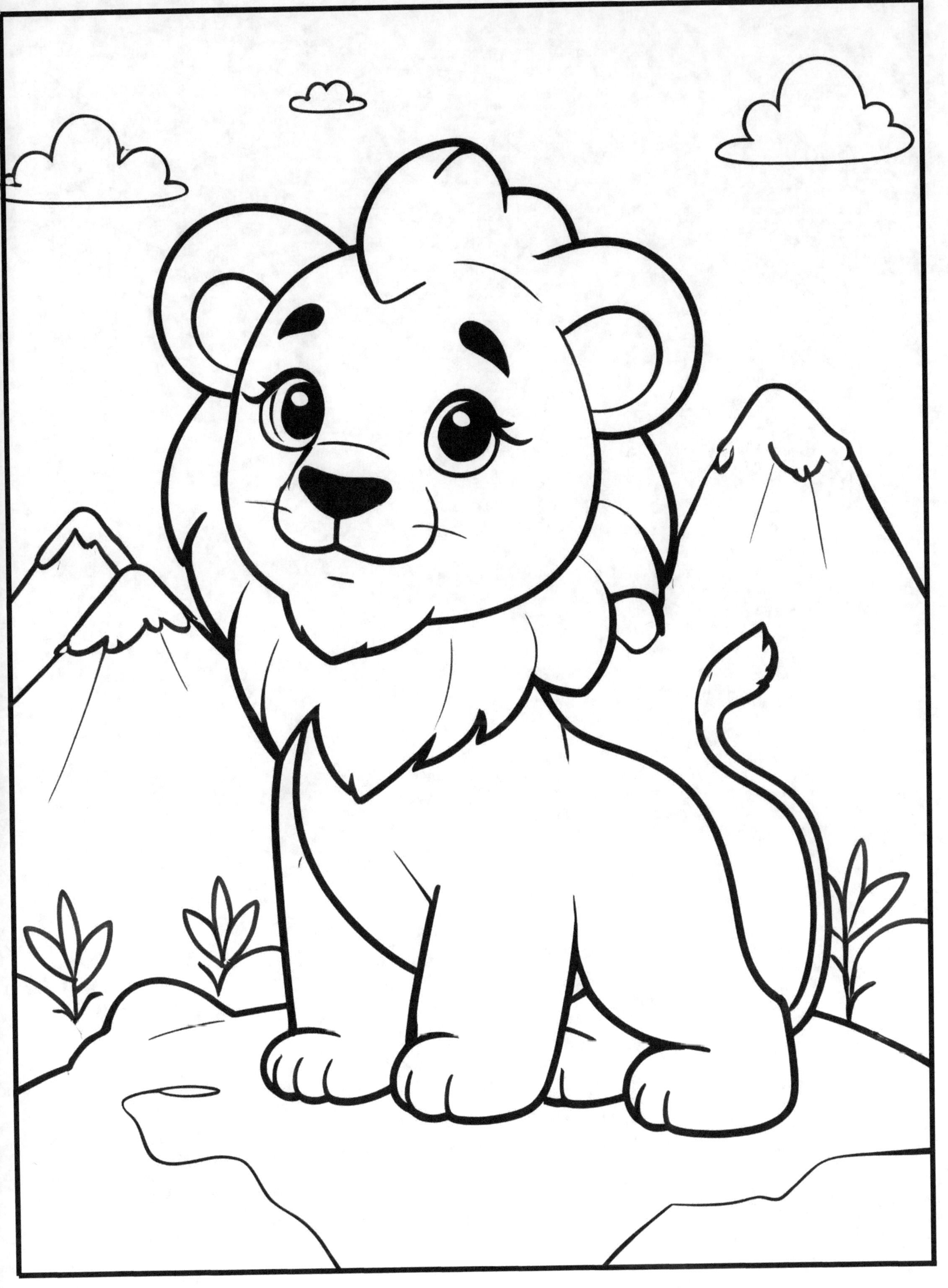